CONTENTS

Introduction 6

Section One: 1900-1914

U.S. and Canada 8: Central and South America 10: Western Europe 12:
Russia and Eastern Europe 14: Japan and the Pacific 16:
Australia and New Zealand 18: China 20: Southern Asia 22:
Africa and the Middle East 24: The Way of the World 26

Section Two: 1914-1918

World War I: Causes 28: World War I: Leaders 30:
World War I: Armies 32: World War I: Civilians 34

Section Three: 1919-1939

The Post-War World 36: U.S. and Canada 38: Central and South America 40:
Western Europe 42: Russia and Eastern Europe 44: Japan and the Pacific 46:
Australia and New Zealand 48: China 50: Southern Asia 52:
Africa 54: The Middle East 56: The Way of the World 58

Section Four: 1939-1945

World War II: Causes 60: World War II: Leaders 62:
World War II: Armies 64: World War II: Civilians 66

Section Five: 1945-1994

Cold War 68: U.S. and Canada 70: South America 72: Western Europe 74:
Former Soviet Union and Eastern Europe 76: Japan and the Pacific 78:
Australia and New Zealand 80: China 82: Southern Asia 84:
Vietnam, Cambodia, and Laos 86: Africa 88: The Middle East 90:
The Way of the World 92

Index 94

Acknowledgments 96

THE CHILDREN'S
Atlas of the 20th Century

THE CHILDREN'S

Atlas of the 20th Century

Chart the century from World War I
to the Gulf War and from "Teddy" Roosevelt
to Nelson Mandela

SARAH HOWARTH

The Millbrook Press
Brookfield, Ct

For Tobie McNeill

A QUARTO BOOK

First published in the United States in 1995 by
The Millbrook Press Inc.
2 Old New Milford Road
Brookfield, Connecticut 06804

Library of Congress Cataloging-in-Publication Data

Howarth, Sarah.
    The children's atlas of the twentieth century / by Sarah Howarth
        p.   cm.
    "A quarto book."
    Includes index.
    Summary: A territorial, social, and political atlas that traces
the changing face of the world this century.
    ISBN 1-56294-885-7 (trade ed.), ISBN 1-56294-563-7 (lib. ed.), ISBN 0-7613-1000-2 (club ed.)
    1. Historical geography – Maps – Juvenile literature.
[1. Historical geography.   2. Atlases.] I. Title
D426.H69   1996
911–dc20   95–12613
                                        CIP
                                         AC

This book was produced by
Quarto Children's Books Ltd
The Fitzpatrick Building
188 – 194 York Way
London N7 9QP

CREATIVE DIRECTOR: Louise Jervis
SENIOR ART EDITOR: Nigel Bradley
EDITOR: Samantha Hilton
PROJECT EDITORS: Molly Perham and Julian Rowe
DESIGN AND PRODUCTION: Glynn Pickerill
and Mick Hodson
MAPS: C. Oakes
PICTURE MANAGER: Sarah Risley
CONSULTANT: Michael Dockrill

Manufactured by Bright Arts (Pty) Singapore
Printed by Star Standard (Pty) Singapore

INTRODUCTION

THE TWENTIETH CENTURY IS A CENTURY OF CHANGES. No part of life is the same now as it was in 1900. In 1900 there were many empires, ruled by powerful kings, queens, and emperors. This pattern of world government was steadily broken. In some places democratic ideals took hold. In other places communist ideas of government were accepted. But the world over, there was a movement toward the idea that everyone could take part in politics – workers, women, ethnic minorities included.

Change has happened more quickly this century than at any other time in history. Science, industry and technology have all played a big part. One miracle invention – the computer – is still revolutionizing the way we live.

A communications revolution means that we can now find out what is happening anywhere in the world in a matter of seconds, using television radio, and satellite. People realize that what takes place in one country can have serious effects on another. Issues like food, health, and pollution all give this important signal.

No one can know what will happen next in the history of the human race. But the idea that each human being has power to improve the world is a hopeful message. It means that big adventures are still to come.

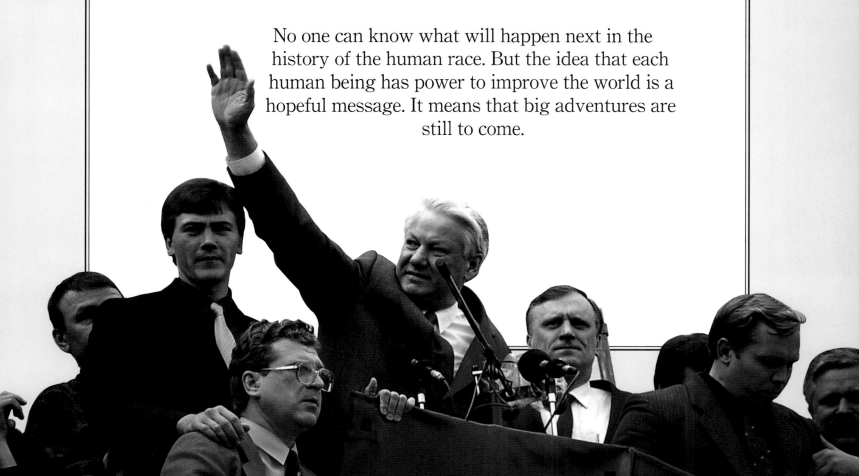

U.S. AND CANADA

THE DAWN OF THE 20TH CENTURY was an exciting time to be alive in North America. Canada was expanding rapidly: two vast new provinces, Alberta and Saskatchewan, were added in 1905. Thousands of immigrants from Europe swelled the labor force. Output from the mines increased and great quantities of wheat and timber were available for export. The economy of the United States was expanding rapidly and the country was in the forefront of technological advance. Oil was struck in Texas in 1901.

Foreign affairs

Following the war with Spain in 1898, the United States gained the Philippines, Guam, and Hawaii in the Pacific, as well as extending her influence in the Caribbean. America was becoming a world power and, as a result, more involved in global problems, especially under President Theodore Roosevelt (1901––1909). Toward Europe, however, the United States remained more detached.

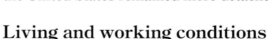

▲ *This family of immigrants from Europe are seeing their new homeland of Canada for the first time.*

Living and working conditions

Progress was made in social affairs. Roosevelt introduced "trust-busting" laws to limit the power of big businesses, and labor laws improved conditions for the workers. In 1910 the National Association for the Advancement of Colored People was set up. The status of women was improved by the Nineteenth Amendment to the Constitution (1919), which gave them the vote for the first time.

▲ *Theodore Roosevelt sought to improve the lives of ordinary Americans. His cousin, Franklin D. Roosevelt, shown here, continued the fight in his presidency 30 years later.*

▼ *On March 15, 1910, the Lakeview No 1 gusher well in Midway Fields at Maricopa, California, started to produce oil. A total of nine million barrels of oil came from the well.*

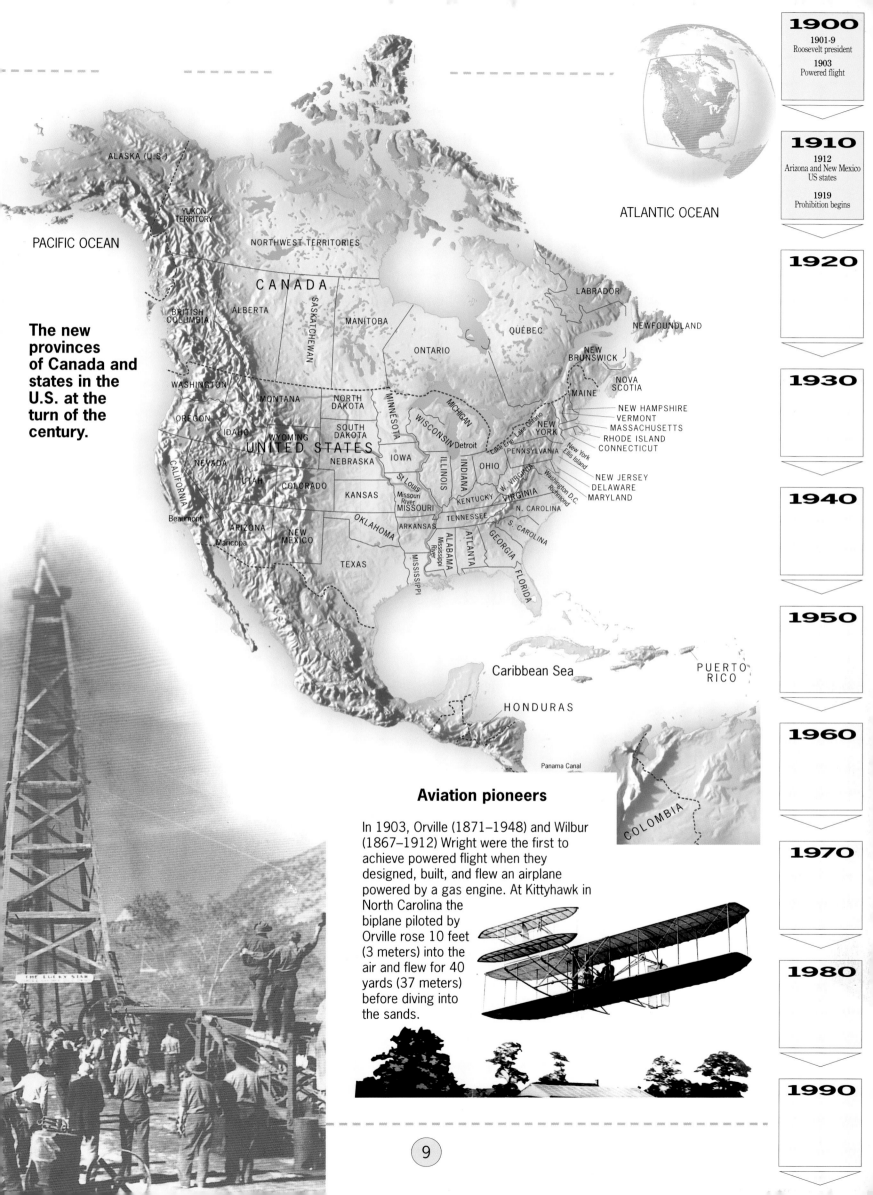

The new provinces of Canada and states in the U.S. at the turn of the century.

PACIFIC OCEAN

ATLANTIC OCEAN

ALASKA (U.S.)

YUKON TERRITORY

NORTHWEST TERRITORIES

CANADA

BRITISH COLUMBIA

ALBERTA

SASKATCHEWAN

MANITOBA

ONTARIO

QUÉBEC

LABRADOR

NEWFOUNDLAND

NEW BRUNSWICK

NOVA SCOTIA

MAINE

NEW HAMPSHIRE
VERMONT
MASSACHUSETTS
RHODE ISLAND
CONNECTICUT

WASHINGTON

OREGON

IDAHO

MONTANA

NORTH DAKOTA

SOUTH DAKOTA

MINNESOTA

WISCONSIN

MICHIGAN

Detroit

Lake Erie Lake Ontario

NEW YORK

New York Ellis Island

UNITED STATES

NEVADA

UTAH

WYOMING

NEBRASKA

IOWA

ILLINOIS

INDIANA

OHIO

PENNSYLVANIA

NEW JERSEY
DELAWARE
MARYLAND

CALIFORNIA

COLORADO

KANSAS

St Louis

Missouri River

MISSOURI

KENTUCKY

W. VIRGINIA

VIRGINIA

Washington D.C.
Richmond

Beaumont

ARIZONA

NEW MEXICO

OKLAHOMA

ARKANSAS

TENNESSEE

N. CAROLINA

Maricopa

TEXAS

MISSISSIPPI

Mississippi River

ALABAMA

ATLANTA

GEORGIA

S. CAROLINA

FLORIDA

Caribbean Sea

PUERTO RICO

HONDURAS

Panama Canal

COLOMBIA

Aviation pioneers

In 1903, Orville (1871–1948) and Wilbur (1867–1912) Wright were the first to achieve powered flight when they designed, built, and flew an airplane powered by a gas engine. At Kittyhawk in North Carolina the biplane piloted by Orville rose 10 feet (3 meters) into the air and flew for 40 yards (37 meters) before diving into the sands.

1900
1901-9
Roosevelt president
1903
Powered flight

1910
1912
Arizona and New Mexico
US states
1919
Prohibition begins

1920

1930

1940

1950

1960

1970

1980

1990

CENTRAL AND SOUTH AMERICA

B Y 1900 CENTRAL AND South America had won political independence from Europe. During the 19th century nationalist forces fought and defeated Spain and Portugal, their old colonial rulers. But although political freedom was won, powerful economic links still tied South America to foreign countries.

Agriculture and industry

South America was rich in natural resources and agricultural products, and overseas demand for exports like bananas, oil, silver, tin, rubber, and coffee helped the economies to grow. Brazil exported its coffee to the world; Argentina sent grain and meat; Chile produced nitrates and copper. Oil was discovered in Venezuela in 1914, and by 1920 the country had become the world's leading oil exporter.

Politics

Economic growth took place against a background of social unrest. Military dictators, or "caudillos," were common: Juan Gomez (1864–1935) ruled in Venezuela; José Zelaya in Nicaragua. The activities of dictators like Zelaya sometimes provided external powers with a pretext for intervention.

▲ *Mines like the copper mine shown here were being developed and exploited in the early 1900s. But they were usually developed by foreign companies, and the money they earned did little for the local people.*

◄ *Coffee has been a money-earning crop in South America throughout the 20th century. Most of it is sent abroad to foreign customers, which ties South America to foreign markets. If people overseas bought less coffee, trade suffered.*

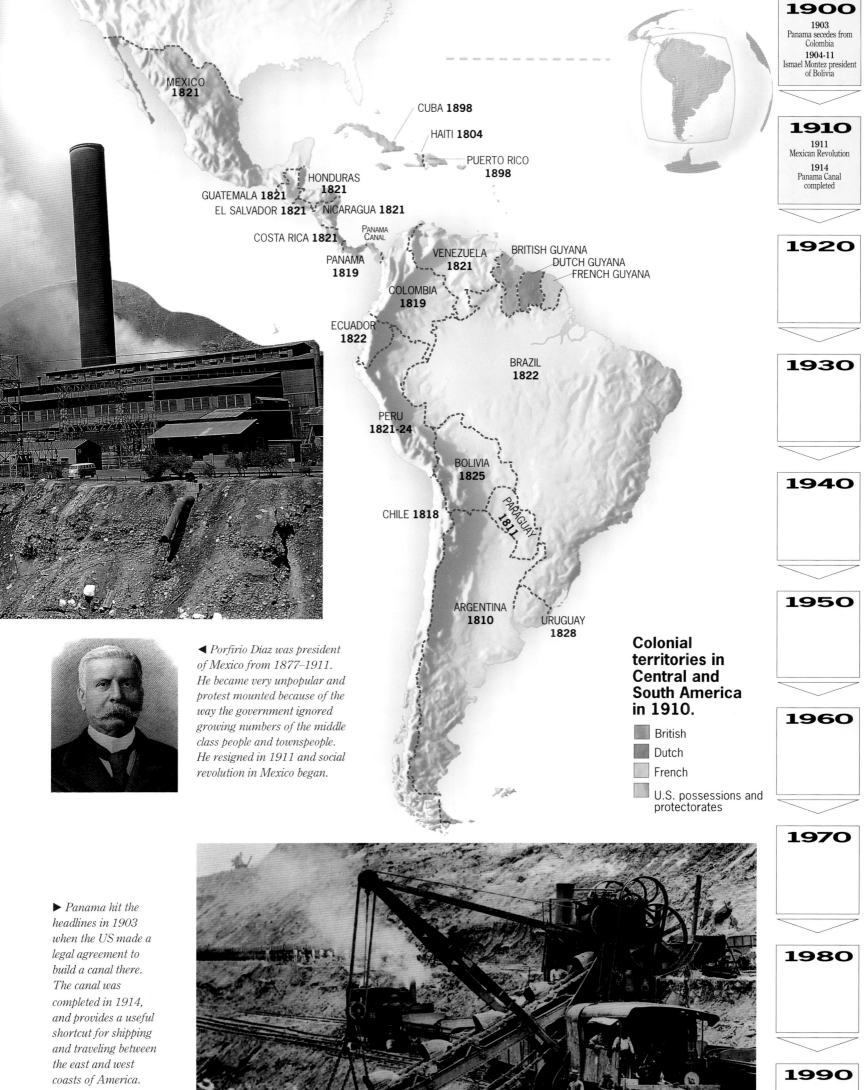

MEXICO **1821**

CUBA **1898**

HAITI **1804**

PUERTO RICO **1898**

HONDURAS **1821**

GUATEMALA **1821**

EL SALVADOR **1821** NICARAGUA **1821**

COSTA RICA **1821**

PANAMA CANAL

PANAMA **1819**

VENEZUELA **1821**

BRITISH GUYANA
DUTCH GUYANA
FRENCH GUYANA

COLOMBIA **1819**

ECUADOR **1822**

BRAZIL **1822**

PERU **1821-24**

BOLIVIA **1825**

PARAGUAY **1811**

CHILE **1818**

ARGENTINA **1810**

URUGUAY **1828**

1900
1903
Panama secedes from Colombia
1904-11
Ismael Montez president of Bolivia

1910
1911
Mexican Revolution
1914
Panama Canal completed

1920

1930

1940

1950

1960

1970

1980

1990

◀ *Porfirio Díaz was president of Mexico from 1877–1911. He became very unpopular and protest mounted because of the way the government ignored growing numbers of the middle class people and townspeople. He resigned in 1911 and social revolution in Mexico began.*

Colonial territories in Central and South America in 1910.

■ British
■ Dutch
■ French
■ U.S. possessions and protectorates

▶ *Panama hit the headlines in 1903 when the US made a legal agreement to build a canal there. The canal was completed in 1914, and provides a useful shortcut for shipping and traveling between the east and west coasts of America.*

WESTERN EUROPE

INDUSTRIAL REVOLUTION WAS BORN in Western Europe, beginning in Britain in the 1700s. In coal, iron, and textiles, Britain dominated the industrial world until the late 1800s. By 1900 rapid growth in the United States and in Germany brought economic rivalry. Steam power was still important, and output from the coal mines was vital, but Germany led the way in the new areas of chemicals and electricity. Precision engineering and experiments with new technology paved the way for further developments, and here, too, Germany was in the lead.

The need for social reform

Rapid population growth provided workers for industry. The Ruhr and Saar in Germany; the north, Midlands, and London in Britain; and also Belgium – all witnessed phenomenal growth.

The housing and living conditions of the working people packed into urban centers was poor, but the start of the 20th century saw greater government concern over social issues.

In Britain, the end of an era came when Queen Victoria, who had been sovereign since 1837, died in 1901.

▲ *Queen Victoria (1819–1901) was crowned Queen of the United Kingdom and Ireland in 1837. She became Empress of India in 1876.*

▲ *Marie Curie of France (1867–1934) studied radioactivity. She and her husband, Pierre, were jointly awarded the Nobel Prize for Physics in 1903. In 1906, Marie Curie became Professor of Physics at the Sorbonne in Paris, France. She was awarded the Nobel Prize for Chemistry in 1911.*

The arts and science

Developments in science, technology, art, and architecture also pointed the way ahead. Artists such as Piet Mondrian (1872–1944) of the Netherlands painted the abstract pictures of the future. The use of geometric design was also a feature of the Bauhaus, a school of art founded at Weimar in Germany in 1919.

▲ *The Italian inventor Guglielmo Marconi (1874–1937) was at the forefront of a communications revolution: radio telegraphy. In 1901, Marconi broke new ground by successfully sending a signal in Morse code from Britain to Canada using radio waves. He later set up radio stations throughout the world to send and receive radio waves.*

▶ *More and more people worked in industry in western Europe at this time, and they began to fight for better pay and conditions. Strike action was one of the ways that newly militant workers' unions sought to bring about change. French railwaymen, miners, and sailors all protested in this way.*

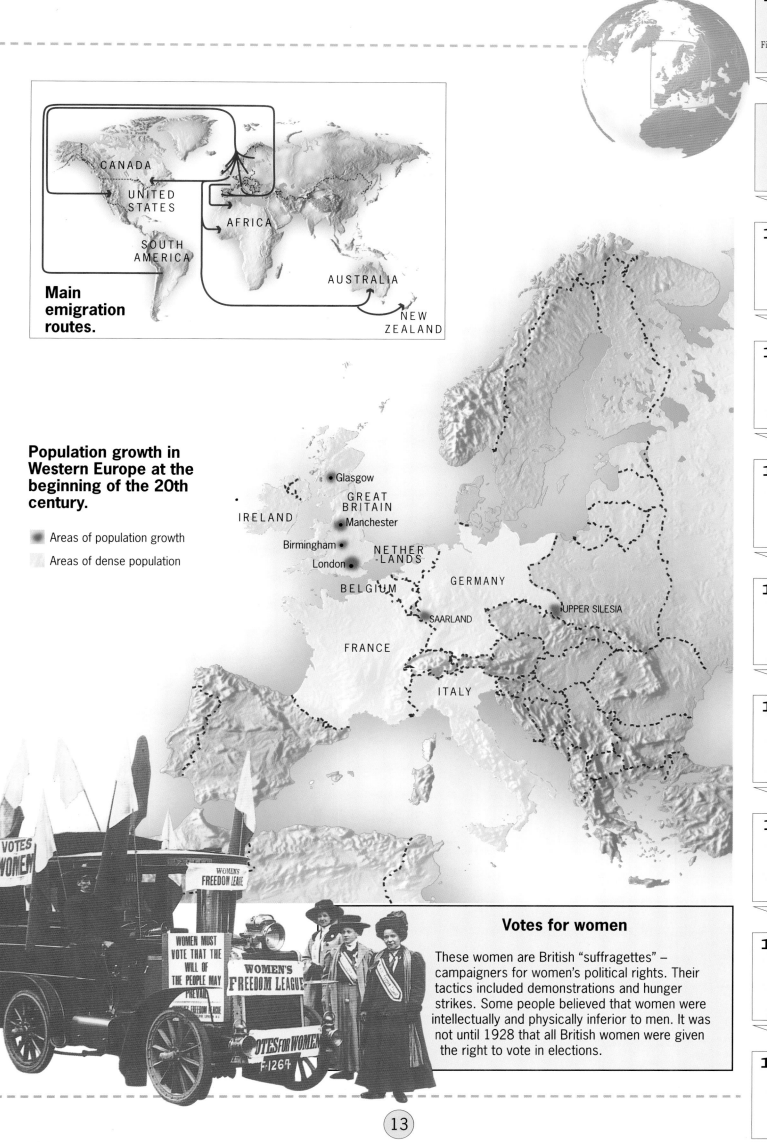

1900
1901
Queen Victoria died
1901
First transatlantic radio
signal

1910
1910
Monarchy ends in
Portugal

1920

1930

1940

1950

1960

1970

1980

1990

Main emigration routes.

CANADA

UNITED STATES

SOUTH AMERICA

AFRICA

AUSTRALIA

NEW ZEALAND

Population growth in Western Europe at the beginning of the 20th century.

Areas of population growth

Areas of dense population

Glasgow

GREAT BRITAIN

IRELAND

Manchester

Birmingham

NETHER-LANDS

London

BELGIUM

GERMANY

SAARLAND

UPPER SILESIA

FRANCE

ITALY

VOTES WOMEN

WOMENS FREEDOM LEAGUE

WOMEN MUST VOTE THAT THE WILL OF THE PEOPLE MAY PREVAIL

WOMEN'S FREEDOM LEAGUE

VOTES FOR WOMEN
F-1264

Votes for women

These women are British "suffragettes" – campaigners for women's political rights. Their tactics included demonstrations and hunger strikes. Some people believed that women were intellectually and physically inferior to men. It was not until 1928 that all British women were given the right to vote in elections.

RUSSIA AND EASTERN EUROPE

IN RUSSIA AND EASTERN EUROPE there were great contrasts between the way people lived. They were greatest in the Russian Empire, where most people were peasants who worked the land in grim poverty. Wealth and power traditionally belonged to the Czar and the aristocracy. But industrial growth during the 1890s created a new community – a working population living in towns. This working class (called the "proletariat" by contemporaries) increased as towns, factories, and railroads expanded.

▲ *Life was hard for many ordinary people in Eastern Europe during this period of uncertainty and political change.*

Political change

Rural and urban unrest grew in this setting. Fueled by Russia's defeat in war against Japan (1904–5), discontent spilled over into revolution in 1905, when serious riots in the capital, St. Petersburg, forced Czar Nicholas II (1894–1917) to grant a parliament or "duma." Political protest in Russia became a strong force, even though it had little official outlet under the Czar's authoritarian rule. Some voices were extreme, such as the Bolsheviks, who supported the views of the political thinker, Karl Marx. They stated that Russia needed violent revolution.

▲ *Karl Marx (1818–83) was a German social, political, and economic theorist. His work led to international communism.*

The road to war

Wealthy landowners and peasant poverty were to be found in other parts of the empires of Eastern Europe. So, too, was a patchwork of different ethnic communities. Nationalism was a growing force. In 1908 Austria annexed the former Ottoman province of Bosnia-Herzegovina, populated by Slavs and controlled by Serbia. Terrorist attacks followed. In 1914, the murder of Archduke Ferdinand, the heir to the Austro-Hungarian throne, by a Serbian-backed terrorist in Sarajevo sparked off World War I.

◀ *Discontent was growing steadily in Russia. Defeat in the war with Japan in 1905 brought matters to a head and revolution broke out. This is a group of pro-Czarist reactionaries.*

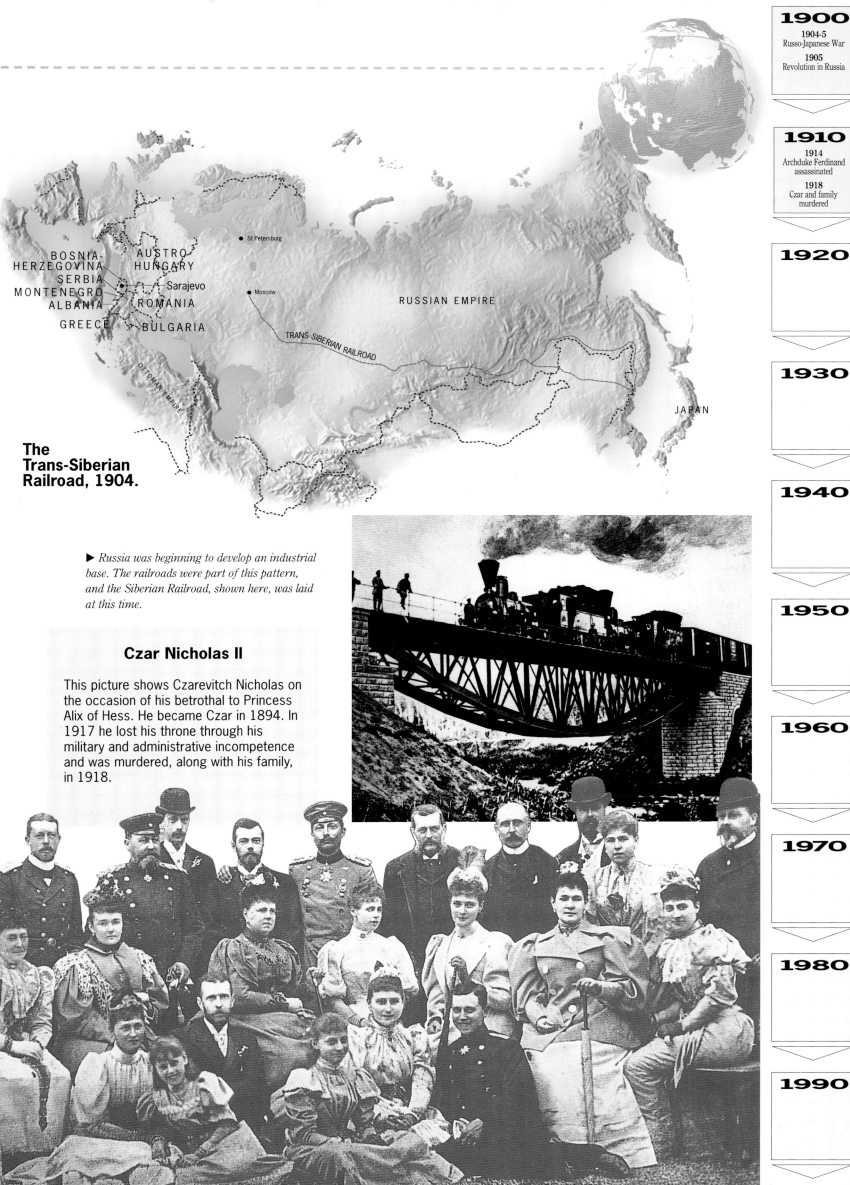

The
**Trans-Siberian
Railroad, 1904.**

1900
1904-5
Russo-Japanese War
1905
Revolution in Russia

1910
1914
Archduke Ferdinand
assassinated
1918
Czar and family
murdered

1920

1930

1940

1950

1960

1970

1980

1990

▶ *Russia was beginning to develop an industrial
base. The railroads were part of this pattern,
and the Siberian Railroad, shown here, was laid
at this time.*

Czar Nicholas II

This picture shows Czarevitch Nicholas on
the occasion of his betrothal to Princess
Alix of Hess. He became Czar in 1894. In
1917 he lost his throne through his
military and administrative incompetence
and was murdered, along with his family,
in 1918.

JAPAN AND THE PACIFIC

AT THE BEGINNING OF THE 20TH CENTURY, JAPAN was modernizing fast. Before, Japan's economy had depended on agriculture, but by 1914 it had become a modern industrial country, using the West as its model. The manufacture of cotton textiles was a major industry. Heavy industry, such as ship building, iron, and steel, was also developed rapidly. The population mushroomed in cities like Osaka and Tokyo. A close-knit railroad network provided a good system of communications.

New policies

The drive to modernize began in the mid-19th century, when the United States, with the rest of the world, imposed trading links on Japan. In 1868, the trade treaties prompted a revolution in government known as the "Meiji restoration", To bring social and economic change, Western-style government bodies were set up, and mass education was sponsored. The privileges of feudal-style samurai warriors were abolished. A navy was founded and a conscript army was established.

▲ The Japanese Emperor Mutsuhito came to power in 1868 (the Meiji restoration). During Mutsuhito's reign Japan was modernized along Western lines.

Military ambition

It was not long before Japan flexed its military muscle. Because the country was poor in natural resources like oil and coal, Japan was eager to gain a foothold in places that could provide raw materials for Japanese industry.

Korea and Manchuria beckoned. Here Japan faced a rival: Russia, too, had imperialistic plans for these territories. War between Russia and Japan followed in 1904–5. Victory brought Japan interests in Manchuria and South Sakhalin (Karafuto). Korea became a Japanese protectorate and was annexed in 1910.

▼ Supplies being unloaded at Dalny, Manchuria, during the Russo-Japanese War of 1905. They were then sent by rail to Japanese 2nd Army HQ outside Port Arthur.

These victories increased Japan's standing in the world community immensely. Few people had dreamed that a non-Western country could defeat a great Western power like Russia. Japan's victory gave heart to other countries, like China, whose people felt pressured by the colonial ambitions of the West.

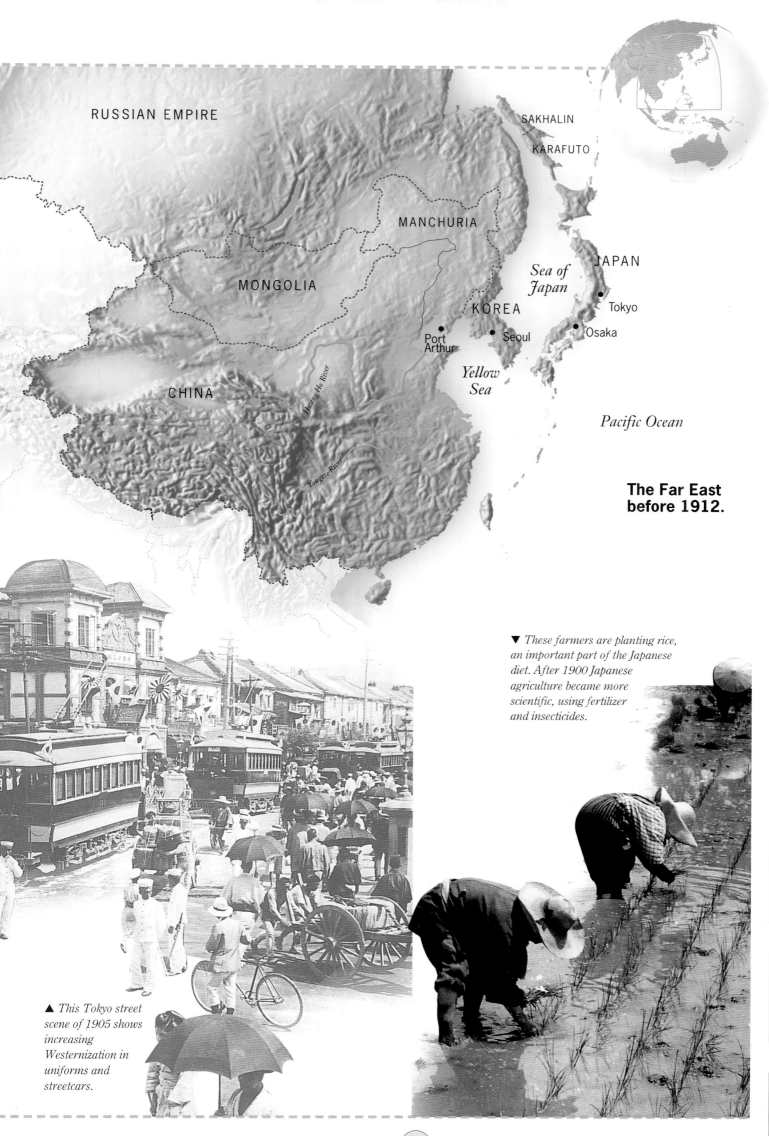

RUSSIAN EMPIRE

SAKHALIN

KARAFUTO

MONGOLIA

MANCHURIA

JAPAN

Sea of Japan

KOREA

• Tokyo

Port Arthur

• Seoul

• Osaka

CHINA

Hwang Ho River

Yellow Sea

Yangtze River

Pacific Ocean

The Far East before 1912.

▼ *These farmers are planting rice, an important part of the Japanese diet. After 1900 Japanese agriculture became more scientific, using fertilizer and insecticides.*

▲ *This Tokyo street scene of 1905 shows increasing Westernization in uniforms and streetcars.*

1900
1904-5
Russo-Japanese War

1910
1910
Japan annexed Korea
1914
Japan entered
World War I

1920

1930

1940

1950

1960

1970

1980

1990

AUSTRALIA AND NEW ZEALAND

IN 1900 GOVERNMENT AND POLITICS were being opened up to the people in Australia and New Zealand. More people could now vote and New Zealand proved itself a world leader when women were given the vote in 1893. Australian women had to wait until 1902. These were pioneering and revolutionary steps. Among men, too, the vote was more widespread than in Europe. "Bush democracy" was growing. So, too, was a Labor movement.

▲ *Australian sheep provided much of the world's wool.*

▲ *Mining for gold and other raw materials provided Australia with valuable export earnings and employment. In the 19th century, the miners' working conditions were very harsh.*

Industrial welfare

Many industries, including mining, crafts, and even sheep shearing, began their own workers' unions. Australia's first Labor government was formed in 1904. In New Zealand, a party promoting the welfare of industrial workers was set up in 1913. Both countries pursued social welfare schemes. Australia introduced pensions for the elderly and invalids in 1909.

Constitutional change

There was change, too, in the way that Australia and New Zealand were governed. Australia, home of the Aborigines, and home to white settlers from the late 1700s, set up the Commonwealth of Australia in 1901. As part of the British Empire, Australia recognized British influence in defense and foreign affairs. New Zealand, also a British colony, was given greater independence, and in 1907 became a dominion in the British Commonwealth.

Mining and agriculture

Agriculture was aimed at overseas customers. Wool, wheat, and refrigerated meat played a major role. Britain was a key market. Mining in Australia provided another source of wealth to export. The export market made the main ports on the coast important, but the pattern of Australian settlement was sketchy. By 1890, two-thirds of the population lived in urban areas, such as Melbourne.

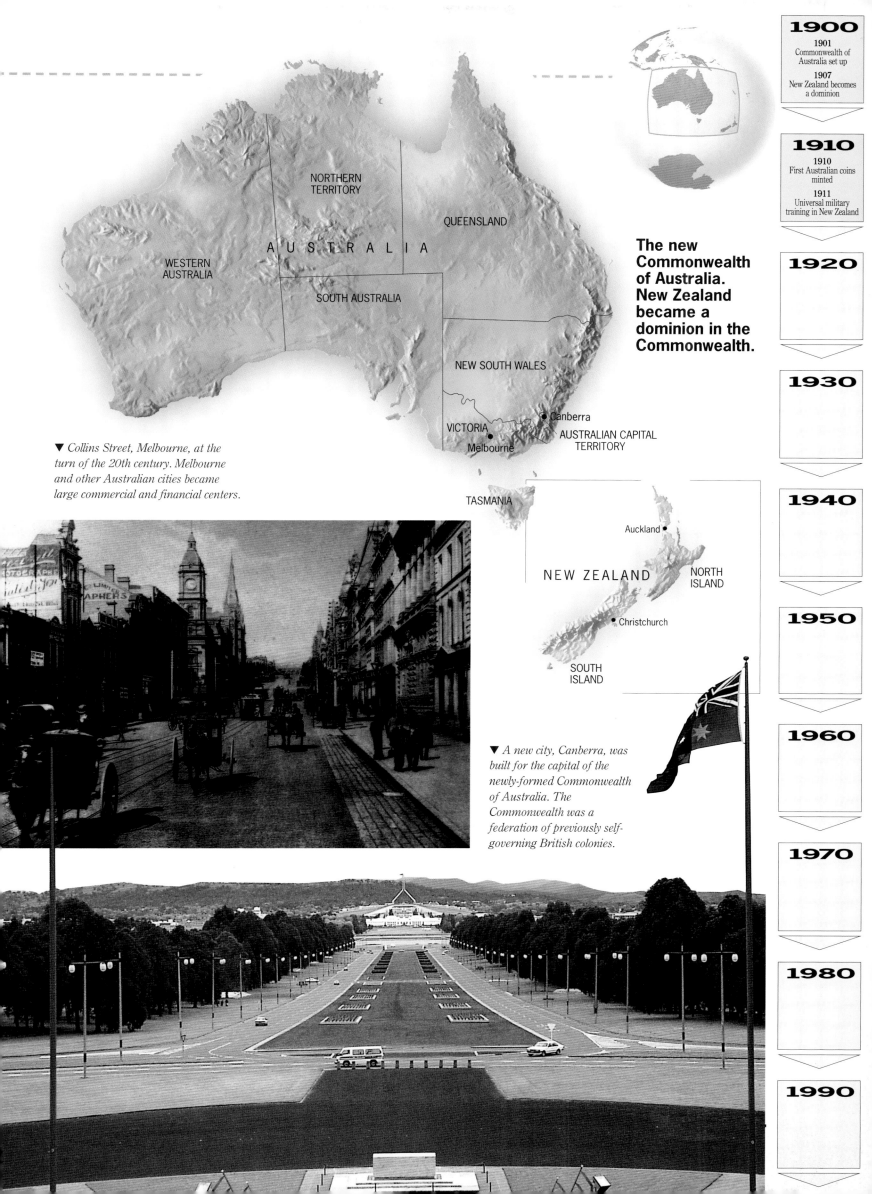

NORTHERN TERRITORY

QUEENSLAND

AUSTRALIA

WESTERN AUSTRALIA

SOUTH AUSTRALIA

NEW SOUTH WALES

VICTORIA

Canberra

AUSTRALIAN CAPITAL TERRITORY

Melbourne

TASMANIA

Auckland

NEW ZEALAND

NORTH ISLAND

Christchurch

SOUTH ISLAND

The new Commonwealth of Australia. New Zealand became a dominion in the Commonwealth.

▼ *Collins Street, Melbourne, at the turn of the 20th century. Melbourne and other Australian cities became large commercial and financial centers.*

▼ *A new city, Canberra, was built for the capital of the newly-formed Commonwealth of Australia. The Commonwealth was a federation of previously self-governing British colonies.*

1900
1901
Commonwealth of Australia set up
1907
New Zealand becomes a dominion

1910
1910
First Australian coins minted
1911
Universal military training in New Zealand

1920

1930

1940

1950

1960

1970

1980

1990

CHINA

THE FIRST YEARS OF THE 20TH CENTURY saw China break with a way of government that had lasted since before the Christian era. China had been an empire for over a thousand years. It was proud of its civilization and closed to influence from other countries. In the 1700s, it was a crime for a foreigner to even learn Chinese.

▲ *For many centuries, China took pride in its distinctive civilization. Many troops sent against the Boxer rebels secretly sympathized with them.*

▼ *Boxer rebels hit out at centers of foreign influence. Overseas officials became a target. This picture shows the British Embassy in Peking besieged by Boxer rebels.*

Foreign influence

Change began in the mid-19th century as first Britain, then other powers, forced China to agree to the presence of foreign traders. Based in Hong Kong, and "treaty ports" such as Xiamen, Fuzhou, Ningbo, and Shanghai, traders and residents established communities free from Chinese control.

The presence of foreigners brought loss of face to the Manchu dynasty that ruled China. Rural unrest, already simmering, boiled over in a series of rebellions. The peasant Taiping rebellion (1851–64) was suppressed. Over 25 million people died in rebellions and upheavals.

In foreign affairs, China was forced to cede territory and make economic concessions to Britain, Russia, France, and Japan.

Imperialism ends

The imperial court confronted a dilemma. Some pushed for modernization and Westernization. They met with failure. In the backlash against Western style reforms, the Boxers, an anti-Western Chinese movement (1898–1900) attacked foreigners, missionaries, and the officials of foreign governments working in China. Reaction was swift. Foreign forces relieved Peking. China was forced to pay a large indemnity to the occupying powers. Nationalism grew in the face of defeat. "Asia for the Asians" became the watchwords. Tired of the Manchu dynasty watching as the once proud Chinese Empire fell to pieces, Chinese nationalists swept away the imperial government. A republic was set up in 1912. Sun Yat-sen (1866–1925) became president at Nanking. Unrest and civil war followed.

▼ *Houseboats in the port of Canton. Ports such as Canton were centers of foreign influence.*

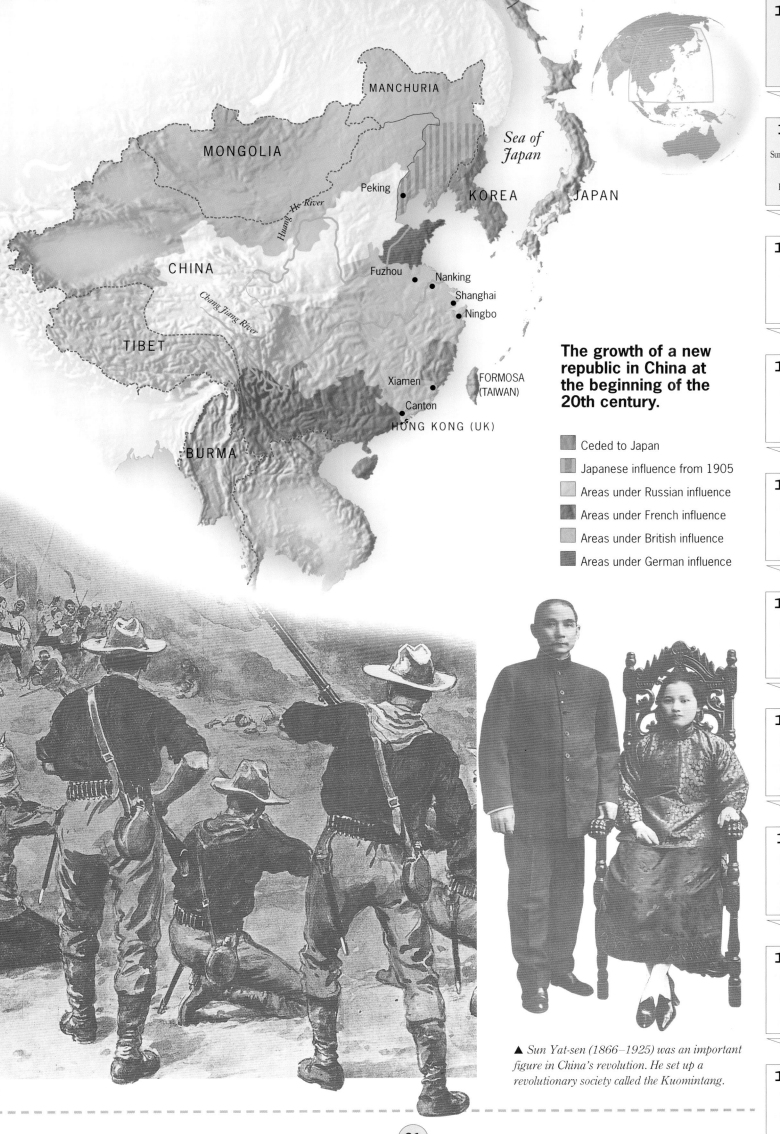

MANCHURIA

MONGOLIA

Sea of
Japan

Huang He River

Peking •

KOREA JAPAN

CHINA

Fuzhou •
Chang Jiang River   • Nanking
                         • Shanghai
TIBET   • Ningbo

Xiamen •   FORMOSA
                (TAIWAN)
Canton •
HONG KONG (UK)

BURMA

The growth of a new republic in China at the beginning of the 20th century.

Ceded to Japan

Japanese influence from 1905

Areas under Russian influence

Areas under French influence

Areas under British influence

Areas under German influence

▲ *Sun Yat-sen (1866–1925) was an important figure in China's revolution. He set up a revolutionary society called the Kuomintang.*

1900
1898-1900
Boxer Revolution
1908
Death of Chinese
Emperor

1910
1911
Sun Yat-sen president of
Chinese Republic
1912
Kuomintang set up

1920

1930

1940

1950

1960

1970

1980

1990

SOUTHERN ASIA

INDIA WAS THE "JEWEL IN THE CROWN" of the British Empire. It was a country of great diversity, where traditional rural life existed beside pockets of industrial development. Colonial civil servants lived next to indigenous people. Hindu and Muslim, wealthy and poor, Western-educated and uneducated, supporters of the British Raj (empire) and Indian nationalists, all added their distinctive character.

Industrialization

Agriculture provided an existence for most of the population. But survival was precarious. Famine struck in 1901, leaving over one million dead. Industry gave work to a growing number of people. Textile-producing Bombay was especially important. Most large-scale economic enterprises were financed by Britain, as was railroad construction. Railroads bound the country together.

▲ *A high-ranking member of the British Army sits with a group of Indian chiefs.*

▲ *The Indian economy began to change as Indian-owned industry developed. The Tata Iron and Steel Company seen here operated in Bihar.*

The rise of nationalism

Political change was in the air. Nationalist feeling began to create tension in many parts of Asia. In Indo-China, the French faced resistance and terrorism. In Sumatra, the Dutch fought indigenous forces. The Indian National Congress was founded in 1885, with the aim of winning a greater share for Indians in the Indian government. The Muslim League, founded in 1906, put forward Muslim views. Feeling crystallized over the issue of dividing the province of Bengal in 1905. Here conflict between Hindu and Muslim played a part, the division creating a Hindu majority in West Bengal and a Muslim majority in East Bengal. In response, Britain gave Indians a small share in local government in 1909.

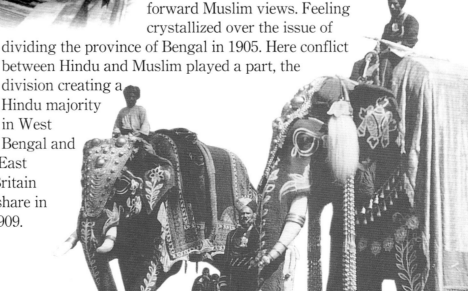

▶ *Poverty and wealth lived side by side in colonial India. These elephants belonged to the wealthy circle of the Maharajah of Mysore.*

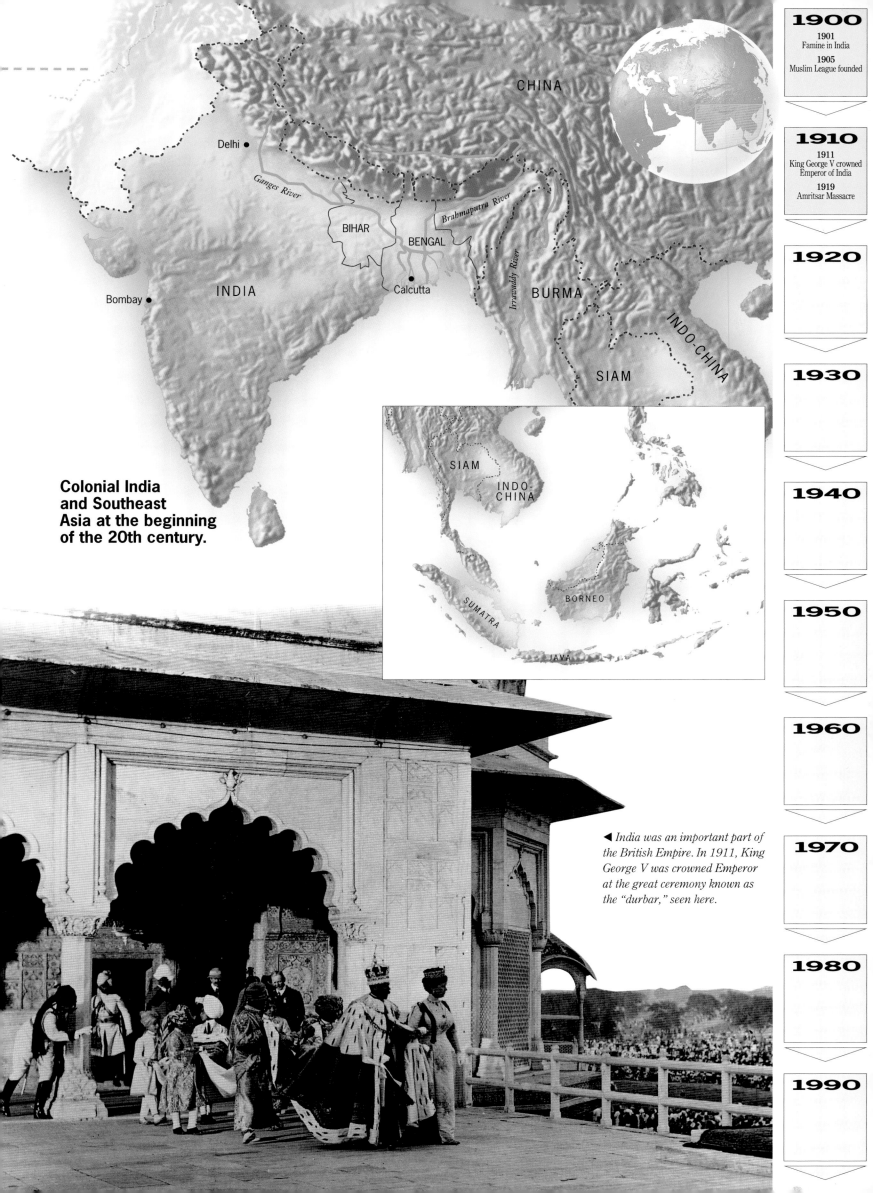

Colonial India and Southeast Asia at the beginning of the 20th century.

CHINA

Delhi

Ganges River

BIHAR

Brahmaputra River

BENGAL

Calcutta

INDIA

Bombay

BURMA

Irrawaddy River

SIAM

INDO-CHINA

SIAM

INDO-CHINA

SUMATRA

BORNEO

JAVA

◀ *India was an important part of the British Empire. In 1911, King George V was crowned Emperor at the great ceremony known as the "durbar," seen here.*

1900
1901
Famine in India
1905
Muslim League founded

1910
1911
King George V crowned
Emperor of India
1919
Amritsar Massacre

1920

1930

1940

1950

1960

1970

1980

1990

AFRICA AND THE MIDDLE EAST

FROM ABOUT 1880, the European powers became involved in a scramble to add to their empires. In Africa, ancient borders were redrawn, taking little account of the tribes involved. African colonization ended when Italy seized Libya in 1911 and Ethiopia in 1936. Spain and France divided Morocco in 1912. In the Middle East, British interests in Persia and Egypt were largely economic, based on Persian oil and the desire to protect the Suez Canal, a vital waterway for the passage to India.

▲ *The Masai tribesmen of Kenya were displaced from their lands by British settlers.*

Resistance to colonialism

For the indigenous populations, colonial rule was difficult to accept. Warrior tribes like the Ndebele of Rhodesia, and herdsmen such as the Masai of Kenya, found it especially hard to adapt. In German South-West Africa and Tanganyika (German East Africa) resistance simmered, and there were uprisings in 1904 and 1905. However, ultimately modern military technology – the machine gun – upheld colonial rule. The empire builders fought among themselves, too. Germany was unhappy with its share of overseas colonies, and rivalry with France led to two crises over Morocco, in 1905–1906 and again in 1911. In the Cape region of the south, tension among the white settler communities led to the Boer War of 1899–1902.

Rise of nationalism

National feeling began to find expression in many places. In 1912 the African National Congress (ANC) was established by a Zulu Methodist minister, J. W. Dube, in Bloemfontein. Schools set up by Christian missionaries from Europe helped to spark national feeling and criticism of colonial rule – although that was far from their intention. Islam, too, contributed to the opposition to colonial rule when a pan-Islamic movement began in Turkey in 1908. In Somalia, a Muslim called Sayyid Muhammad led resistance to Britain and Italy, giving Somali tribes a sense of national identity.

▲ *Opened in 1869, the Suez Canal became a vital strategic and commercial lifeline between Britain and India. In 1875 Britain bought the controlling share in the Canal from Egypt.*

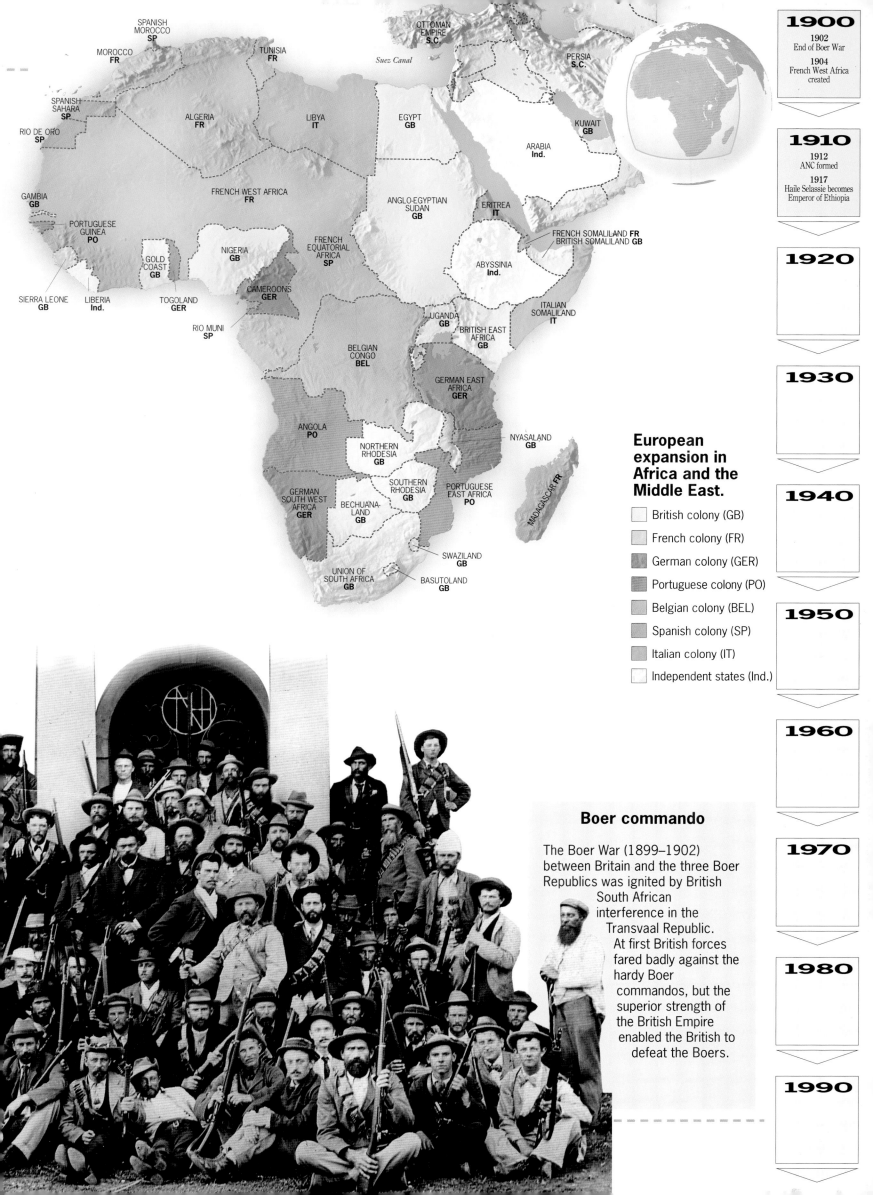

Map labels

SPANISH MOROCCO **SP**
MOROCCO **FR**
TUNISIA **FR**
OTTOMAN EMPIRE **S.C.**
Suez Canal
PERSIA **S.C.**
SPANISH SAHARA **SP**
RIO DE ORO **SP**
ALGERIA **FR**
LIBYA **IT**
EGYPT **GB**
KUWAIT **GB**
ARABIA **Ind.**
GAMBIA **GB**
PORTUGUESE GUINEA **PO**
FRENCH WEST AFRICA **FR**
ANGLO-EGYPTIAN SUDAN **GB**
ERITREA **IT**
FRENCH SOMALILAND **FR**
BRITISH SOMALILAND **GB**
NIGERIA **GB**
GOLD COAST **GB**
FRENCH EQUATORIAL AFRICA **SP**
ABYSSINIA **Ind.**
SIERRA LEONE **GB**
LIBERIA **Ind.**
TOGOLAND **GER**
CAMEROONS **GER**
ITALIAN SOMALILAND **IT**
RIO MUNI **SP**
UGANDA **GB**
BRITISH EAST AFRICA **GB**
BELGIAN CONGO **BEL**
GERMAN EAST AFRICA **GER**
ANGOLA **PO**
NYASALAND **GB**
NORTHERN RHODESIA **GB**
GERMAN SOUTH WEST AFRICA **GER**
BECHUANA-LAND **GB**
SOUTHERN RHODESIA **GB**
PORTUGUESE EAST AFRICA **PO**
MADAGASCAR **FR**
SWAZILAND **GB**
UNION OF SOUTH AFRICA **GB**
BASUTOLAND **GB**

European expansion in Africa and the Middle East.

- ☐ British colony (GB)
- ☐ French colony (FR)
- ☐ German colony (GER)
- ☐ Portuguese colony (PO)
- ☐ Belgian colony (BEL)
- ☐ Spanish colony (SP)
- ☐ Italian colony (IT)
- ☐ Independent states (Ind.)

Boer commando

The Boer War (1899–1902) between Britain and the three Boer Republics was ignited by British South African interference in the Transvaal Republic. At first British forces fared badly against the hardy Boer commandos, but the superior strength of the British Empire enabled the British to defeat the Boers.

Timeline

1900
1902 End of Boer War
1904 French West Africa created

1910
1912 ANC formed
1917 Haile Selassie becomes Emperor of Ethiopia

1920

1930

1940

1950

1960

1970

1980

1990

THE WAY OF THE WORLD

A NEW WORLD, THE MODERN world, was born in the years before World War I (1914–1918). World population grew at a rate never known before, jumping from 900 million to 1,600 million during the 19th century. But growth was not the same the world over: advances in medical treatment and public health, together with adequate food supplies, meant that people living in the most developed parts of the world – Europe and America – had the best chance of reaching old age. It was very much a white man's world, with Europe and America dominating the rest of the globe.

Technical and economic advances
Political and economic links with colonies and less technologically developed countries led to the gradual creation of a world economy. Europe and America were the birthplaces of new developments in industry, science, and technology.

During the 20th century, these transformed much of the world, turning quiet farming communities into busy towns and cities linked together by new rapid transport. In the 1800s, coal, iron, and textiles formed the backbone of industry. In the 1900s there were new industries such as steel, chemicals, and electricity.

Unequal shares
However, for some people the development of the modern world brought grim working conditions, and a far from equal share in the rewards. This was especially true for the people of tropical countries, who provided the crops and commodities required by those living in the West.

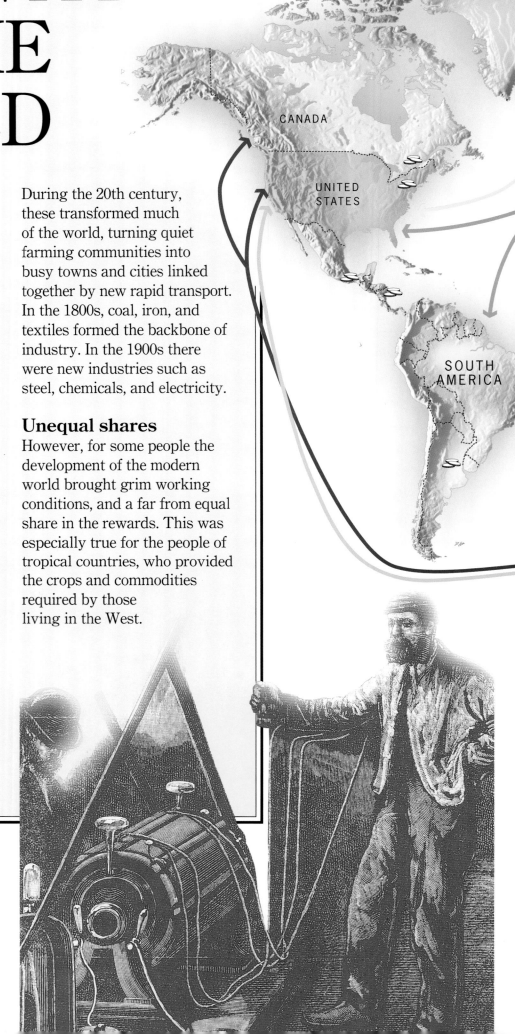

CANADA

UNITED STATES

SOUTH AMERICA

▶ *After 1879 electricity was used for an ever increasing number of functions. In particular, electric lighting gradually replaced gas. This is an early dynamo electric light generator.*

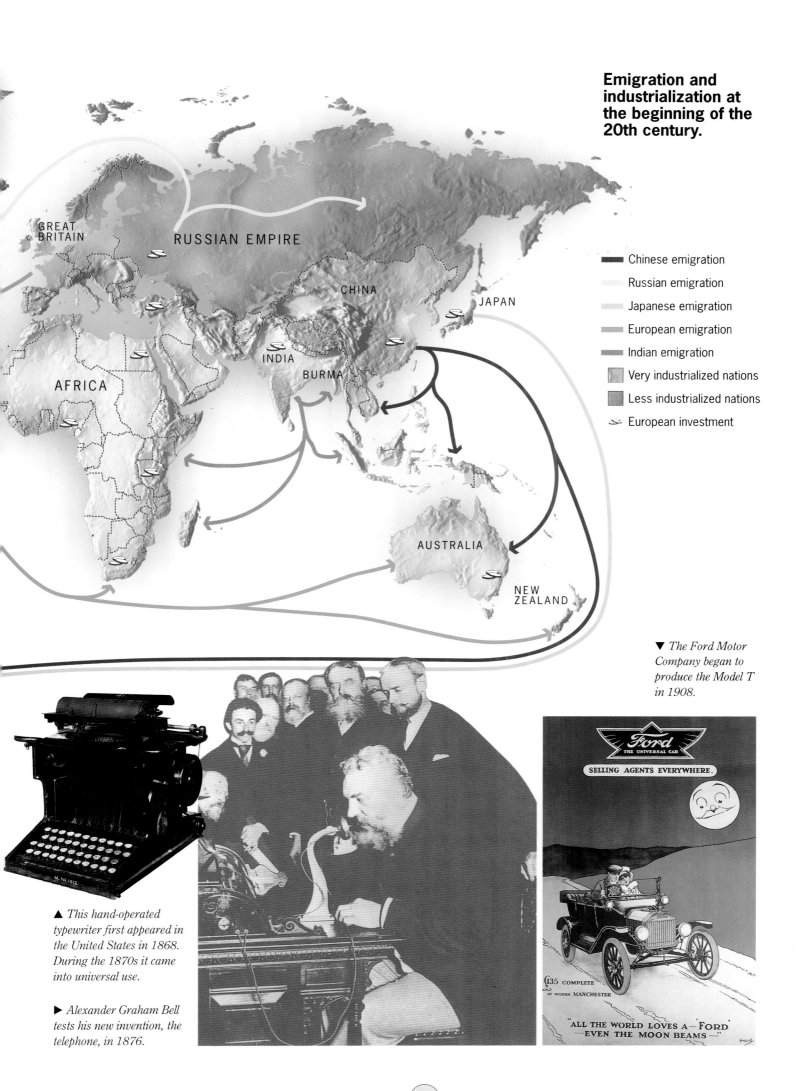

Emigration and industrialization at the beginning of the 20th century.

GREAT BRITAIN

RUSSIAN EMPIRE

CHINA

JAPAN

INDIA

BURMA

AFRICA

AUSTRALIA

NEW ZEALAND

- Chinese emigration
- Russian emigration
- Japanese emigration
- European emigration
- Indian emigration
- Very industrialized nations
- Less industrialized nations
- European investment

▼ *The Ford Motor Company began to produce the Model T in 1908.*

▲ *This hand-operated typewriter first appeared in the United States in 1868. During the 1870s it came into universal use.*

▶ *Alexander Graham Bell tests his new invention, the telephone, in 1876.*

Ford
THE UNIVERSAL CAR

SELLING AGENTS EVERYWHERE.

£135 COMPLETE
AT WORKS MANCHESTER

"ALL THE WORLD LOVES A—FORD
—EVEN THE MOON BEAMS—"

WORLD WAR 1: CAUSES

THE SHOT THAT STARTED THE GREAT WAR OF 1914–1918 was fired in the Bosnian city of Sarajevo, in the Balkans. Its target was Archduke Franz Ferdinand, heir to the throne of the Austro-Hungarian Empire. The assassin was a Serbian student called Gavrilo Princip.

The Balkan crisis

Violence and unrest were not new in the Balkans, which was once part of the Ottoman Empire. Increasingly contested by the great powers – Russia, Austria-Hungary, Italy, Germany, France, and Britain – and home to militant nationalist movements in countries like Serbia, the Balkans had already been the scene of bitter warfare in 1912–1913. There had been friction between Austria and Serbia in particular, especially after Austria's annexation of the Ottoman province of Bosnia-Herzegovina in 1908, which Serbia coveted.

▲ *Soldiers from Montenegro, seen here, increased their territory during the Balkan Wars of 1912 and 1913.*

If a quarrel between Austria-Hungary and Serbia was all that was needed to push the Balkans over the edge into war, then a quarrel in the Balkans was all that the other European powers needed to push them into armed conflict.

Military alliance

In 1914 Russia, Britain, and France stood together as the Triple Entente. Germany and Austria-Hungary had formed their own alliance, pledged to support each other in the event of attack. When put to the test in 1914, these alliances brought the whole of Europe into war.

▲ *Serbian student Gavrilo Princip is arrested in Sarajevo in 1914 for the murder of Austrian Archduke Franz Ferdinand.*

▶ *Archduke Ferdinand at Sarajevo, moments before his death in June 1914. Austria blamed Serbia for his murder.*

Alliances at the start of World War I.

- Allies
- Central Powers

RUSSIA

GREAT BRITAIN

BELGIUM

GERMANY

FRANCE

AUSTRIA-HUNGARY

ROMANIA

BOSNIA-HERZEGOVINA

Sarajevo •

SERBIA

BULGARIA

ITALY

ALBANIA

OTTOMAN EMPIRE

GREECE

▼ *Refugees flee Belgium. In 1914, German armies marched into France by way of Belgium, aiming to take France by surprise.*

Mobilization

Great destructive power was unleashed in World War I as the new industrialized powers of Europe, such as Britain and Germany, produced weapons on a new scale of efficiency. Factories turned out tanks, guns, ammunition, and barbed wire. The railroad network carried troops to the front to fight. Germany realized it could not cope with a war against both France and Russia and aimed to eliminate France before turning on the French ally, Russia. This plan was the brainchild of German General Alfred von Graf Schlieffen (1833–1913).

WORLD WAR 1: LEADERS

ALTHOUGH THE SYSTEM OF ALLIANCES helped to bring different countries into the Great War, there were many reasons for the call to arms. The German Empire under Kaiser Wilhelm II was keen to signal its arrival as a world class power. The Kaiser dismissed the famous Iron Chancellor, Otto von Bismarck, in 1890 and himself played a leading role in pushing Germany forward. With a powerful fleet of Dreadnought battleships masterminded by Naval Commander Admiral Alfred von Tirpitz, Germany entered into a naval arms race with Britain.

France and Britain

France resented the position Germany had built up in Europe, its defeat by Germany in the war of 1870, and the German seizure of Alsace-Lorraine in 1871. Georges Clemenceau (1841–1929) became prime minister in 1917 and was determined to lead France to victory. He appointed the French General Ferdinand Foch (1851–1929) to command the French-British armies in 1918. The British war effort was galvanized by the Welsh politician David Lloyd George (1863–1945), who became prime minister in 1916.

Kaiser Wilhelm II

Kaiser Wilhelm II (1859–1941) ruled Germany during World War I. He had been keen to build Germany up as a military and naval power in the years before 1914. He was an enthusiast of military uniform and loved to wear the British uniforms given to him by his grandmother, Queen Victoria.

Russia and America

Russia fought under Czar Nicholas II and generals such as Aleksey Brusilov (1853–1926). Revolution against the Czar and his ineffectual leadership led eventually to the Bolshevik Revolution in October 1917. The Bolsheviks then took Russia out of the war. America entered the war in 1917 under President Woodrow Wilson (1856–1924).

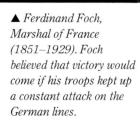

▲ *Ferdinand Foch, Marshal of France (1851–1929). Foch believed that victory would come if his troops kept up a constant attack on the German lines.*

▶ *Nicholas II, last Czar of Russia (1868–1918). He took personal command of Russia's armies in World War I.*

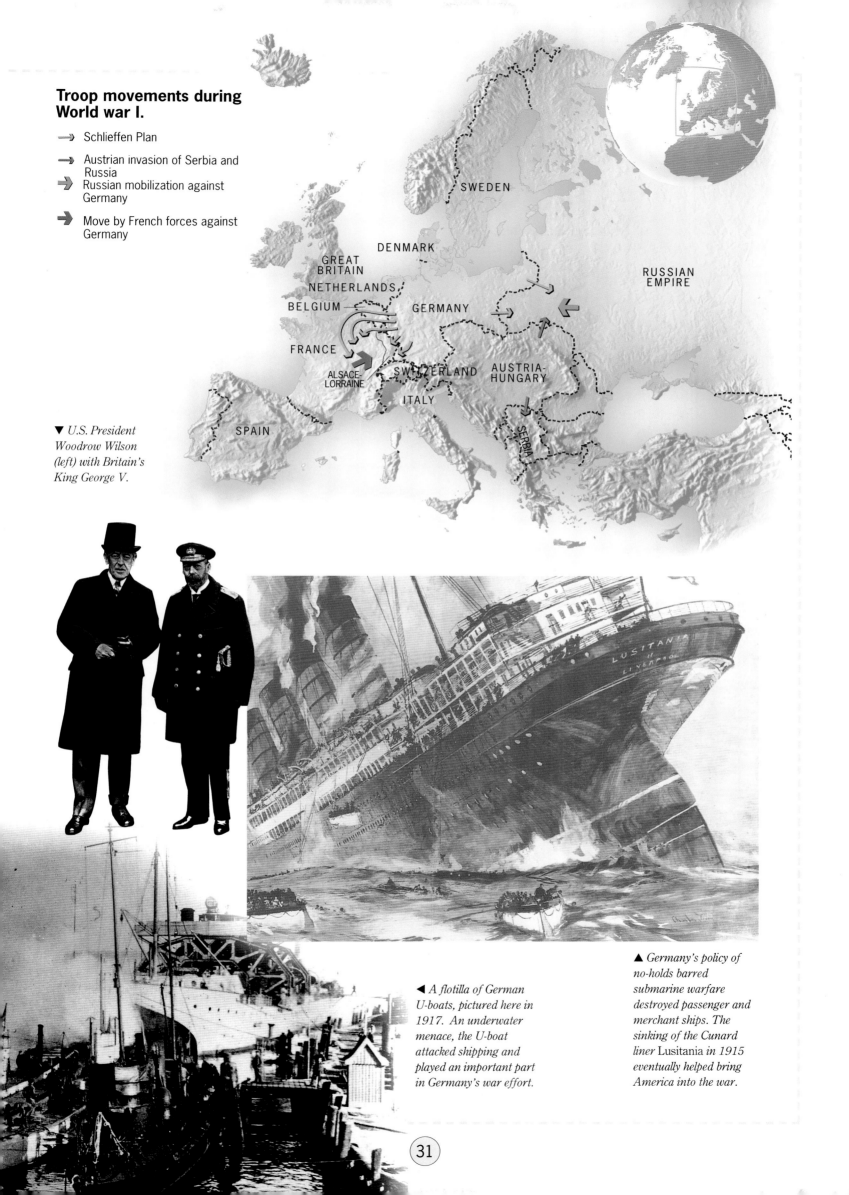

Troop movements during World war I.

→ Schlieffen Plan

→ Austrian invasion of Serbia and
   Russia

⇒ Russian mobilization against
   Germany

➤ Move by French forces against
   Germany

▼ *U.S. President
Woodrow Wilson
(left) with Britain's
King George V.*

SWEDEN

DENMARK

GREAT
BRITAIN

NETHERLANDS

BELGIUM

GERMANY

RUSSIAN
EMPIRE

FRANCE

ALSACE-
LORRAINE

SWITZERLAND

AUSTRIA-
HUNGARY

ITALY

SERBIA

SPAIN

◄ *A flotilla of German
U-boats, pictured here in
1917. An underwater
menace, the U-boat
attacked shipping and
played an important part
in Germany's war effort.*

▲ *Germany's policy of
no-holds barred
submarine warfare
destroyed passenger and
merchant ships. The
sinking of the Cunard
liner* Lusitania *in 1915
eventually helped bring
America into the war.*

WORLD WAR I: ARMIES

"**H**OME BY CHRISTMAS!" That was the optimistic cry as the armies of the European powers marched to war, flags flying, crowds cheering, in July and August 1914. Everyone expected that the war would mainly be fought – and won – in Western Europe. Germany followed the Schlieffen Plan, the strategy mapped out by the German Chief of the Army General Staff, General Alfred von Graf Schlieffen, before the war. The German army marching into France through Belgium would destroy the French army from the rear. Then switching the bulk of her armies from the west to the east, Germany would crush the Russian army, whose mobilization would take longer to organize than the French forces.

▲ *Trench warfare meant long spells in the trenches, with bursts of activity as men were sent "over the top" to attack the enemy.*

Trench warfare

The plan failed. There was no knock-out blow. Instead, the opposing sides dug grimly into their positions. This was the Western Front, a line of fortifications linking the Swiss border to the English Channel. The story of war here was one of stalemate, trench warfare, and sporadic offensives by infantry on enemy positions defended by barbed wire, artillery, and machine guns. These were the bloodbaths of the Somme (1916), Verdun (1916), and Passchendaele (1917). Over half a million men died at Passchendaele alone.

▲ *Troops land at Anzac Cove in the Dardanelles, as part of the Gallipoli campaign, 1915–16.*

▼ *War in the air employed planes and airships. This was a new element to combat.*

Global conflict

The Allies failed to defeat the Ottoman Empire in the Gallipoli campaign in 1915, and in Mesopotamia, Arabia, and Palestine until 1917 and 1918. War came to Africa and the Pacific, where German colonies were seized by Japan and Britain. The impact of war was felt worldwide as imperial powers like Britain drew on troops from India, Africa, Australia, and New Zealand. War was given a new and terrifying face by the use of poison gas, machine guns, and tanks. German U-boats destroyed Allied shipping, and planes and airships took conflict into the air.

The battles and fronts of World War I.

- ● Important battles
- ▬ The Western Front
- ▬ The Eastern Front

Jutland **1916**

DENMARK

RUSSIAN EMPIRE

GREAT BRITAIN

NETHERLANDS

Tannenberg **1914** ● ● Masurian Lakes **1914**

GERMANY

Ypres **1914** and **1915**

BELGIUM

Passchendaele **1917**

Somme **1916**

Marne **1914**

Verdun **1916**

SWITZERLAND

Caporetto **1917**

AUSTRIA-HUNGARY

FRANCE

Vittorio Veneto **1918**

ITALY

ROMANIA

SERBIA

BULGARIA

SPAIN

ALBANIA

Dardanelles

Gallipoli **1915**

GREECE

OTTOMAN EMPIRE

PALESTINE

EGYPT

ARABIA

▶ *The use of tanks was limited at first, but military leaders gradually recognized that they could help bring an end to the stalemate in the trenches.*

WORLD WAR I: CIVILIANS

"I WANT YOU!" This was the slogan of army recruiting posters in the United States. In Britain, the pointing finger of Lord Kitchener (1850–1916) carried the same message. For the first time, war spilled over into civilian life. Governments demanded massive civilian help as well as military mobilization to fight "total war."

Providing food, arms, ammunition, uniforms, transport, and everything else needed by armies at war meant that governments directed economic affairs to an extent not known before. In Germany, industrialist Walther Rathenau (1867–1922) helped organize raw materials and industrial production for the government. In Britain, Lloyd George brought businessmen into partnership to help run the war effort.

The home front

All sections of the population had to be mobilized behind the government. Women

▲ *This picture of a female dispatch rider illustrates the range of duties in which women were engaged.*

moved into traditional male jobs as munitions workers, mechanics, drivers, in industry, offices, transport – almost everywhere there was a gap to fill. Workers were persuaded to put national interests first. Disputes about wages and conditions were largely held back until war-weariness and general disillusionment, price increases, and food shortages took hold by 1917.

Civilian casualties

Violence touched civilian life. Refugees fled occupied countries like Belgium. Air raids brought bombs to Britain and Germany. Germany's strategy of no-holds-barred submarine warfare destroyed Allied and neutral passenger and merchant ships alike. The sinking of the Cunard liner, *Lusitania,* off the coast of Cork, Ireland in 1915, showed how politics blurred the divide between soldier and non-combatant in time of war. Carrying rifle ammunition and shrapnel as well as passengers, the *Lusitania* combined the role of luxury liner and Allied supporter.

▲ *During the war feeling against foreigners ran high. Here a crowd loots a shop belonging to a German family in the East End of London.*

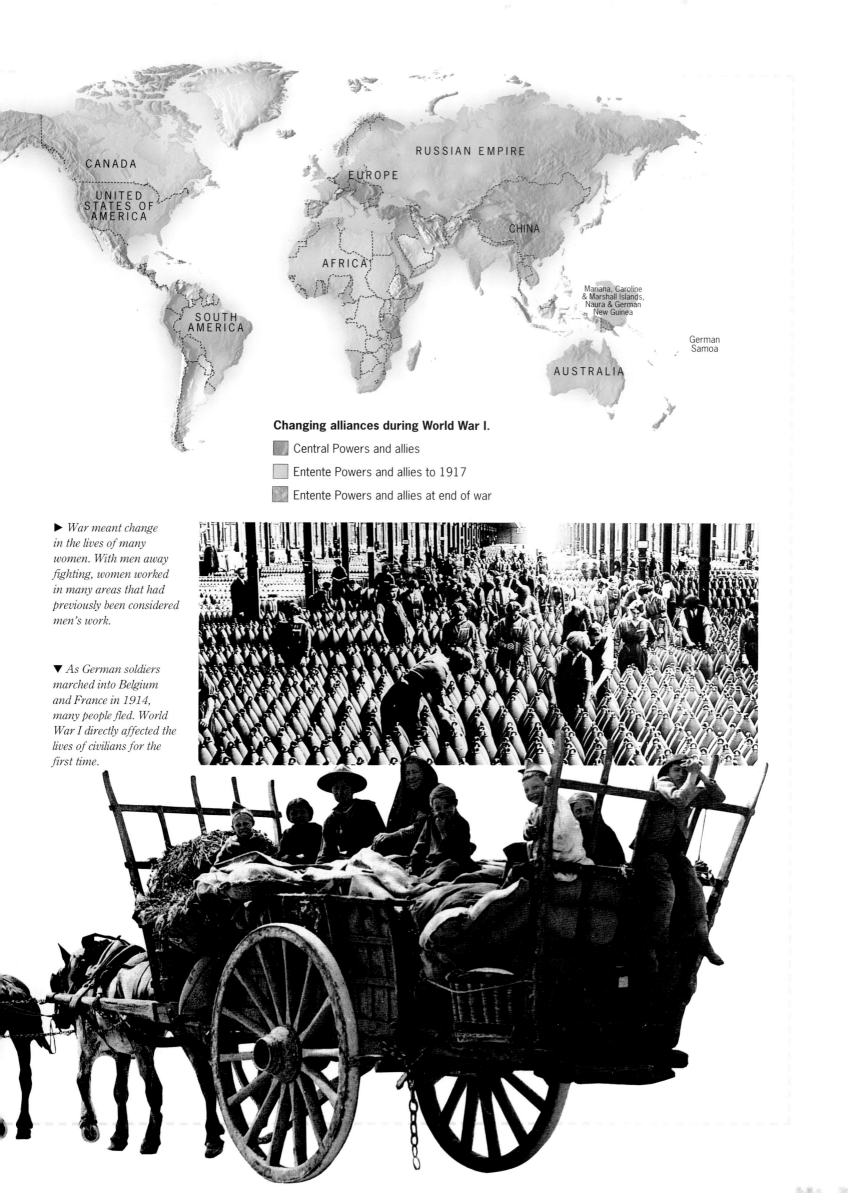

CANADA

UNITED
STATES OF
AMERICA

SOUTH
AMERICA

EUROPE

AFRICA

RUSSIAN EMPIRE

CHINA

Mariana, Caroline
& Marshall Islands,
Nauru & German
New Guinea

German
Samoa

AUSTRALIA

Changing alliances during World War I.

Central Powers and allies

Entente Powers and allies to 1917

Entente Powers and allies at end of war

▶ *War meant change in the lives of many women. With men away fighting, women worked in many areas that had previously been considered men's work.*

▼ *As German soldiers marched into Belgium and France in 1914, many people fled. World War I directly affected the lives of civilians for the first time.*

THE POST-WAR WORLD

Germany

THE END OF THE FIRST global war brought global problems to the peace table. In the negotiations between the victors in Paris in 1919, Woodrow Wilson of the United States, Georges Clemenceau of France, and David Lloyd George of Britain dominated. The Treaty of Versailles brought peace with Germany and the map of Europe was redrawn. The Ottoman, Russian, and Austro-Hungarian empires were dissolved.

In their place, a number of new states were created. These included Finland, Estonia, Poland, Czechoslovakia, and Yugoslavia, which were all republics.

Germany had to accept drastic reductions in her military strength and pay massive compensation for war damages she had inflicted on the Allies. The Rhineland was made a demilitarized zone and France re-took Alsace and Lorraine, seized by Germany in 1871. Poland was created out of former Russian, German, and Austrian territory.

New problems

In the Middle East, the Ottoman Empire lost most of its territory. Syria and Lebanon went to France; Palestine, Iraq, and Saudi Arabia to Britain. These territories were "mandates," to be prepared for self-government, watched over by the newly-formed League of Nations. The British promise of support for a Jewish homeland in Palestine, 1917, brought unrest almost immediately among the Arab population.

The peace settlement was widely seen as victory for democracy over the old powers of empire. But many problems remained. Although the new European map tried to follow ethnic boundaries, this was not always possible. Economic problems like inflation soon added to the tension. Outside Europe, the power of empire still clung. India was disappointed not to receive greater political freedom for its war aid to the British. In many parts of Asia and Africa the social and economic changes brought by war added to nationalist feeling.

▼ *Economic instability and the Franco-Belgian occupation of the Ruhr created runaway inflation in Germany in 1923. Here, a German child plays with worthless bundles of banknotes.*

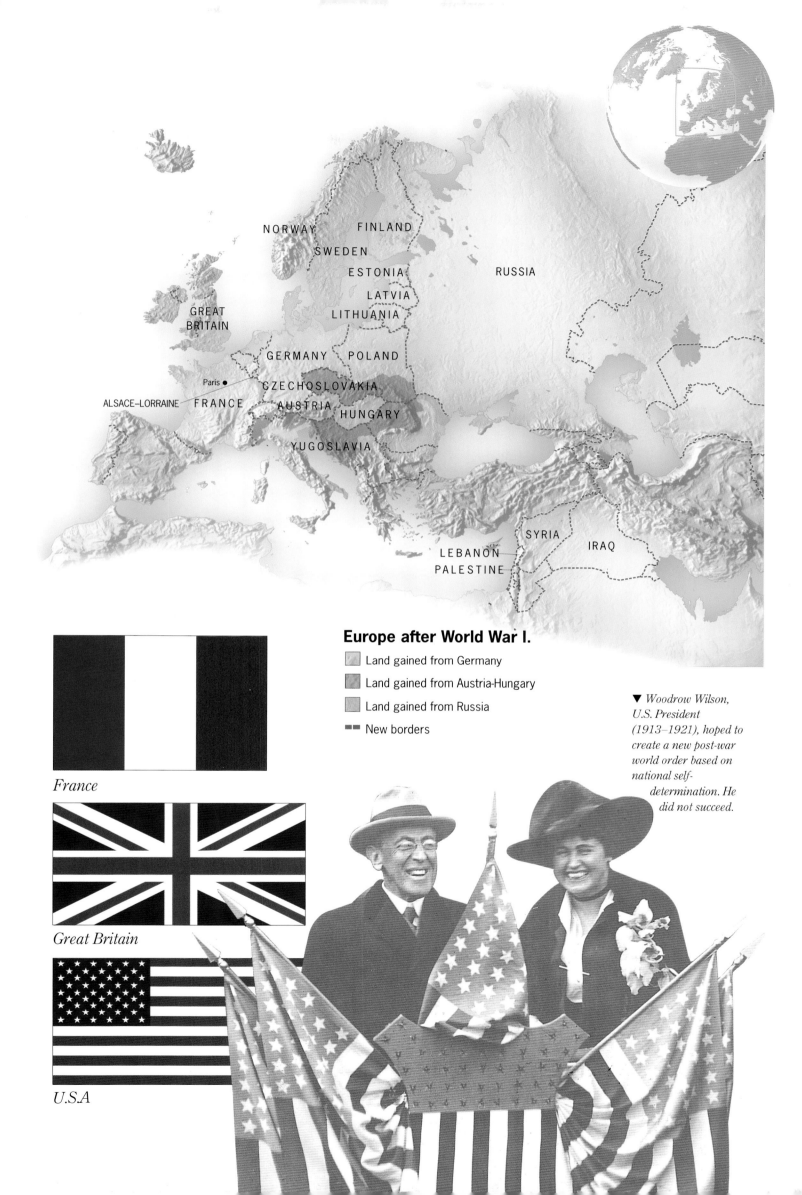

NORWAY
FINLAND
SWEDEN
ESTONIA
RUSSIA
LATVIA
LITHUANIA
GREAT
BRITAIN
GERMANY POLAND
Paris ●
CZECHOSLOVAKIA
ALSACE–LORRAINE FRANCE
AUSTRIA
HUNGARY
YUGOSLAVIA
SYRIA
IRAQ
LEBANON
PALESTINE

Europe after World War I.
▨ Land gained from Germany
▨ Land gained from Austria-Hungary
▨ Land gained from Russia
▬▬ New borders

France

Great Britain

U.S.A

▼ *Woodrow Wilson,*
U.S. President
(1913–1921), hoped to
create a new post-war
world order based on
national self-
determination. He
did not succeed.

U.S. AND CANADA

THE 1920s AND 1930s IN THE UNITED STATES were years of great contrast. The country seemed to reach dizzying heights of prosperity in the 1920s, only to fall to levels of poverty in the 1930s.

New industries in the 1920s brought higher standards of living. The car industry boomed and Detroit became one of the largest cities in the United States. Shares were bought and sold on the New York Stock Exchange, bringing wealth to a wide range of people. Moviegoing became a popular new pastime, as crowds flocked to see films starring Charlie Chaplin, Rudolph Valentino, and Douglas Fairbanks. New dance crazes, such as the Charleston, took off, and there were new styles of popular music as the sound of jazz was heard in cities like New Orleans.

▲ *Prohibition outlawed alcohol. Here New York State troopers unload boxes of confiscated alcohol in 1921.*

▼ *Welfare tried to reach out to those hit by the Depression, as lines formed for free soup and other aid.*

The Great Depression

But there was a dark side to life, too. In 1919 "Prohibition" – the outlawing of liquor trading – began. Underground trade soon sprang up, bringing crime and racketeering to the streets. Chicago suffered from the activities of gangsters like Al Capone. Then, in 1929, the New York Stock Exchange on Wall Street crashed. Throughout North America, shares and savings became worthless, industry slumped, banks closed, and people were out of work. This bleak outlook continued into the 1930s, giving this period the name the "Great Depression." The crisis was made worse by drought and storms that reduced farmland to a "dust bowl," and ruined many farmers. A new president, Franklin D. Roosevelt, was elected in 1932 to get the United States out of crisis. His "New Deal" measures created employment opportunities and helped to reduce the worst features of the Depression. Despite the times, some familiar U.S. landmarks went up in the 1930s – San Francisco's Golden Gate Bridge and New York City's Empire State Building.

FREE COFFEE & DOUGHNUTS UP FOR THE UNEMPLOYED

FREE SOUP

▶ *Louis "Satchmo" Armstrong (1898–1971) the American jazz trumpeter and singer was the first major jazz virtuoso.*

Crisis and change in post-war North American cities.

CANADA

UNITED STATES OF AMERICA

Ottawa

Chicago

New York

Washington

Detroit

San Francisco

New Orleans

▼ *The Golden Gate Bridge in San Francisco was opened in May 1937.*

Roosevelt's "New Deal" work program

U.S. President Franklin Roosevelt aimed to boost the economy and set up work programs for the unemployed. The Depression hit Canada hard, too. Prime Minister Mackenzie King (1874–1950) passed social legislation such as the National Housing Act of 1938 to try to bring about a brighter future.

1900
1901-9
T. Roosevelt president
1903
First powered flight

1910
1912
Arizona and New Mexico US states
1919
Prohibition begins

1920
1929
Wall Street Crash

1930
1932
F.D. Roosevelt elected president
1933
Tennessee Valley Authority

1940

1950

1960

1970

1980

1990

CENTRAL AND SOUTH AMERICA

THE 1920S AND 1930S BROUGHT upheaval in many Latin American countries. Economic and social change was in the air, fueled in part by the European demand for raw materials during World War I. Countries like Brazil and Mexico, which already had developing economies, particularly experienced change.

Dictatorship

In Bolivia, Mexico, and Brazil revolution brought new governments that were committed to rise up against powerful landlords and dominant foreign business interests. These were "popular dictatorships," supported by the new working class that had grown up in developing cities, by the peasants, and frequently by the army. With such support Daniel Salamanca became president of Bolivia in 1931.

In Brazil, the work of President Getúlio Vargas (president 1930–1937) earned him the nickname "Father of the Poor." As well as raising living standards, he promoted the steel and chemical industries.

Lázaro Cárdenas

President Lázaro Cárdenas sought peaceful revolutionary change for Mexico by redistributing land to the peasantry, nationalizing the railroads and the oil industry, promoting mass education and welfare rights, and championing the labor movement.

Revolution and change

In Mexico, Lázaro Cárdenas (president 1934–1940) was known for his policy of land redistribution, transferring land from wealthy landowners to the peasants. He also nationalized foreign-owned industries such as the railroads and oil, and championed mass education and welfare rights. The spirit of the Mexican revolution was captured by the artist Diego Rivera (1886–1957).

During this period there were frontier disputes between the different countries. The Chaco War (1932–1935) between Bolivia and Paraguay was fought over the Gran Chaco – a plain at the foot of the Andes. In the United States, a new policy of non-intervention in Latin America was termed the "Good Neighbor" policy.

▼ *The Chaco War (1932–1935) between Paraguay and Bolivia was fought over the Gran Chaco plain. Here, Paraguayan troops are transported to the front.*

▲ *Getúlio Vargas (1883–1954) was twice president of Brazil, from 1934–1937 and from 1951–1954. He sought to improve the conditions of the people and encouraged industrialization.*

▼ *Diego Rivera (1886–1957), a Mexican painter of frescoes, painted* Arsenal *to capture the spirit of Mexico's industrial revolution. He revived the fresco technique of classical times.*

La Paz
MEXICO
Mexico City
Atlantic Ocean
HONDURAS
GUATEMALA
Caribbean Sea
EL SALVADOR
NICARAGUA
Lake Nicaragua
Panama Canal
COSTA RICA
Pacific Ocean
PANAMA
VENEZUELA
GUYANA
SURINAM
FRENCH GUIANA
COLOMBIA
ECUADOR
BRAZIL
Amazon
PERU
BOLIVIA
Andes Mountains
PARAGUAY
The Gran Chaco Plains
CHILE
Rio de Janeiro
Asunción
URUGUAY
ARGENTINA

Social upheaval and revolutionary wars in Central and South America.

▼ *In June 1935 the Paraguay-Bolivian armistice ended the Chaco War. The victor, Paraguay, secured most of the Gran Chaco plain in 1938.*

1900
1903
Panama secedes from Colombia
1904-11
Ismael Montez president of Bolivia

1910
1911
Mexican Revolution
1914
Panama Canal completed

1920
1929
National Revolutionary Party formed in Mexico

1930
1934-37
Vargas president of Brazil
1934-40
Cárdenas president of Mexico
1932-5
Chaco War

1940

1950

1960

1970

1980

1990

WESTERN EUROPE

THE SURVIVORS OF THE WAR were determined to bring about change. Workers pressed for greater rights, often using strike action to make their point. Troops were used against strikers in Britain in 1926, but some improvements were made to social welfare. In Britain, new housing estates were built in the suburbs outside London for the newly-prosperous lower middle classes during the 1930s.

▲ *Dr. Marie Stopes (1880–1958), university lecturer, did much to pioneer birth control.*

Social and political change

Women clung to the freedom they had known in wartime. The "new" woman scandalized old-fashioned opinion with a shorter hemline, shorter hair, and make-up; and she even smoked in public! The shadow of violence hung over western Europe. Irish nationalist feeling flowered in a revival of the Gaelic language, as well as in military and political pressure. At Easter in 1916 an uprising in Dublin failed, but in 1922 the tie with Britain was broken with the creation of the Irish Free State. The six north-eastern counties of Ulster remained part of the United Kingdom.

Post-war depression

After the war, economic depression hit living standards, bringing unrest and support for extreme right-wing politics. After 1922, Italy was ruled by the fascist dictator Benito Mussolini (1883–1945). In Germany, the Weimar Republic struggled to cope with inflation and unemployment. There was bitterness when France and Belgium occupied the Ruhr (1923). Adolf Hitler (1889–1945) and the Nazis took power in Berlin in 1933. Civil war broke out in Spain in 1936.

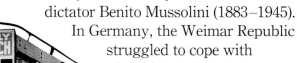
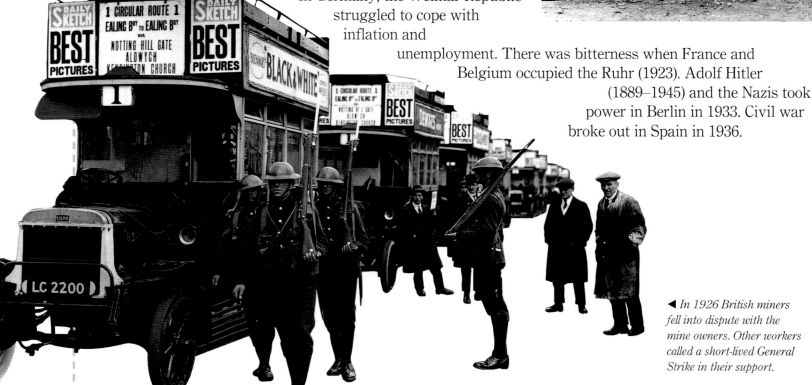

◄ *In 1926 British miners fell into dispute with the mine owners. Other workers called a short-lived General Strike in their support.*

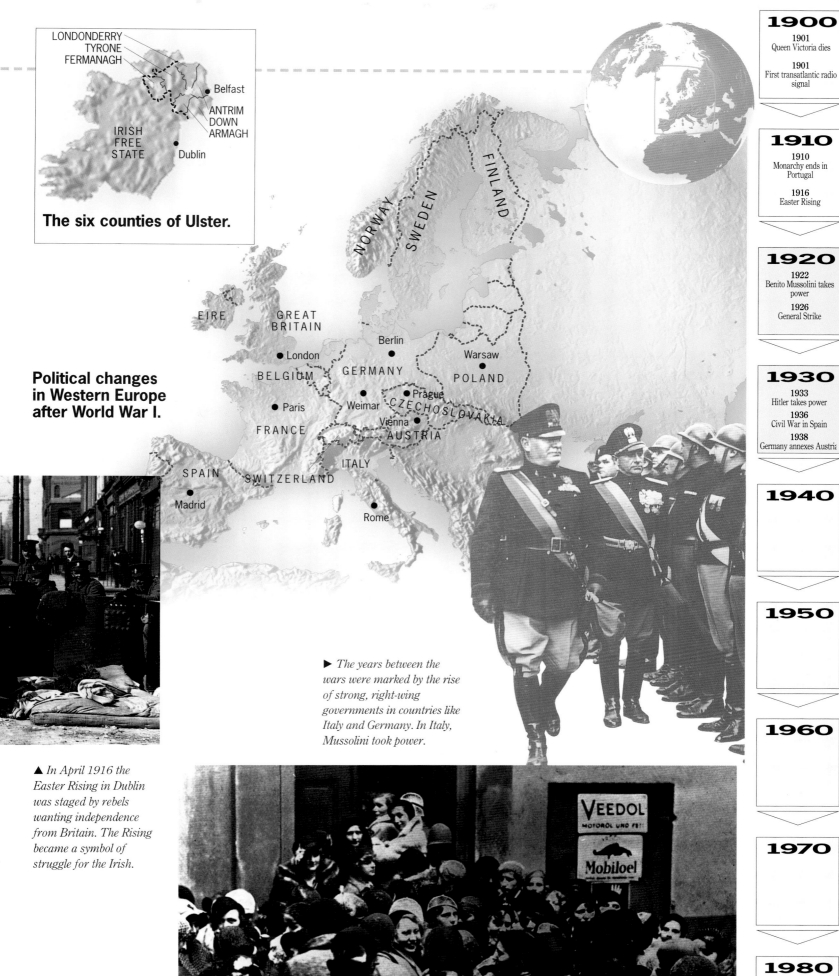

LONDONDERRY
TYRONE
FERMANAGH

Belfast

ANTRIM
DOWN
ARMAGH

IRISH
FREE
STATE

Dublin

The six counties of Ulster.

NORWAY
SWEDEN
FINLAND

**Political changes
in Western Europe
after World War I.**

EIRE

GREAT
BRITAIN

Berlin

London

Warsaw

BELGIUM

GERMANY

POLAND

Paris

Weimar

Prague

CZECHOSLOVAKIA

FRANCE

Vienna

AUSTRIA

SPAIN

SWITZERLAND

ITALY

Madrid

Rome

▲ In April 1916 the
Easter Rising in Dublin
was staged by rebels
wanting independence
from Britain. The Rising
became a symbol of
struggle for the Irish.

► The years between the
wars were marked by the rise
of strong, right-wing
governments in countries like
Italy and Germany. In Italy,
Mussolini took power.

VEEDOL
MOTOROL UND FET

Mobiloel

► Economic crisis and
unemployment shook
Germany after World
War I. Here, hundreds of
Germans are waiting to
apply for one available job.

1900
1901
Queen Victoria dies

1901
First transatlantic radio
signal

1910
1910
Monarchy ends in
Portugal

1916
Easter Rising

1920
1922
Benito Mussolini takes
power
1926
General Strike

1930
1933
Hitler takes power
1936
Civil War in Spain
1938
Germany annexes Austria

1940

1950

1960

1970

1980

1990

RUSSIA AND EASTERN EUROPE

R USSIA WITHDREW FROM WORLD WAR I in 1917 and signed a peace treaty with Germany in 1918, losing much land. The war was unpopular with the Russian people. Vast numbers of peasants had been forced to join the army, leaving the land uncultivated, and shortages of supplies and bad management caused huge losses. Riots broke out in Petrograd and Moscow, and factory workers went on strike. In the countryside, discontented peasants seized land from their landlords.

▲ Lenin led the Bolsheviks to power in the October Revolution of 1917, and ruled Russia until his death in 1924.

Communism

The soldiers who had fought so bravely mutinied and deserted their regiments. Without the support of his army, Czar Nicholas II was forced to leave the throne, and in July 1918 he and his family were assassinated. In October 1917 power passed to the revolutionary leader Vladimir Ilyich Lenin (1870–1924) and the Bolshevik party, who were dedicated communists. Lenin promised "peace, land, bread," but violence continued as war broke out on Russian soil between the Red Army, who supported revolution, and White armies who wanted to maintain the old order. Over 13 million people died in the fighting and ensuing famine.

Joseph Stalin

The Soviet Union was set up in 1922. After Lenin's death, a struggle for power took place between leaders Leon Trotsky (1879–1940) and Joseph Stalin (1879–1953). The winner, Stalin, set five-year targets for industrial expansion. Food shortages were blamed on "kulaks," peasants with larger farms, who were wrongly accused of pushing up food prices. Private farms were abolished and run as cooperatives under State control. This policy of 'collectivization' caused famine and great hardship. Communist parties were set up in many other countries at this time.

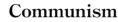

▲ The army lost confidence in the way war was being directed by their leaders. They were among the first to turn against the Czar.

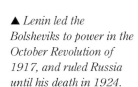

Russia in revolution after World War I.

Area controled by Bolsheviks

Arctic Ocean

SWEDEN

GERMANY

• Petrograd

• Moscow

RUSSIA

Black Sea

Ural Mountains

OTTOMAN EMPIRE

Caspian Sea

JAPAN

CHINA

PERSIA

▼ Russian revolutionaries faced a daunting situation. Poverty and famine existed on a large scale, as this picture clearly shows.

▲ Stalin became the Russian leader in 1924, aiming to transform Russia's economy. Opposition to Stalin was fiercely stamped out.

1900
1905
Revolution in Russia

1910
1914
Archduke Ferdinand assassinated
1918
Czar and family murdered
1917
October Revolution

1920
1924
Stalin came to power
1929
Leon Trotsky exiled

1930
1935
Stalin exiles millions to gulags

1940

1950

1960

1970

1980

1990

JAPAN AND THE PACIFIC

JAPAN ENDED WORLD WAR I on the winning side, gaining possession of former German territory in the Pacific. The Mariana, Caroline, and Marshall Islands were to be ruled as "mandates,": areas under the supervision of the League of Nations. Japanese control in China caused bitter feeling among the Chinese.

An imperial power

A new Japanese emperor, Hirohito (1901–1989), came to the throne in 1926. His reign was known in Japan as the "Showa era," the era of bright peace. Yet the years before World War II (1939–1945) were far from peaceful: two prime ministers were assassinated, and in 1936 extremists in the army staged a bid for power.

After 1931, Japan pursued a policy of aggression and attacked Chinese troops at Mukden. The Japanese took possession of Manchuria and set up a puppet government there, renaming the area Manchukuo. War with China broke out in 1937, after an incident at the Marco Polo Bridge, near Peking, and lasted until 1945. Military spending went up significantly.

Recession and war

Business and agriculture in Japan were badly hit by the recession of the late 1920s and 1930s. As Japan came out of recession, trade with Asian countries such as Korea and Taiwan gradually began to replace part of the trade with Europe and America. Industry developed fast, and in return for hard work and loyalty to the firm, employers provided lifetime employment and good wages. When war broke out in 1941, Japan switched to a total war economy.

▲ *Japanese Emperor Hirohito's reign (1926–1989) saw dramatic changes in Japan's fortunes. After 1931 Japan became increasingly militaristic, expanding into Manchuria and North China. In 1941 Japan went to war with the West.*

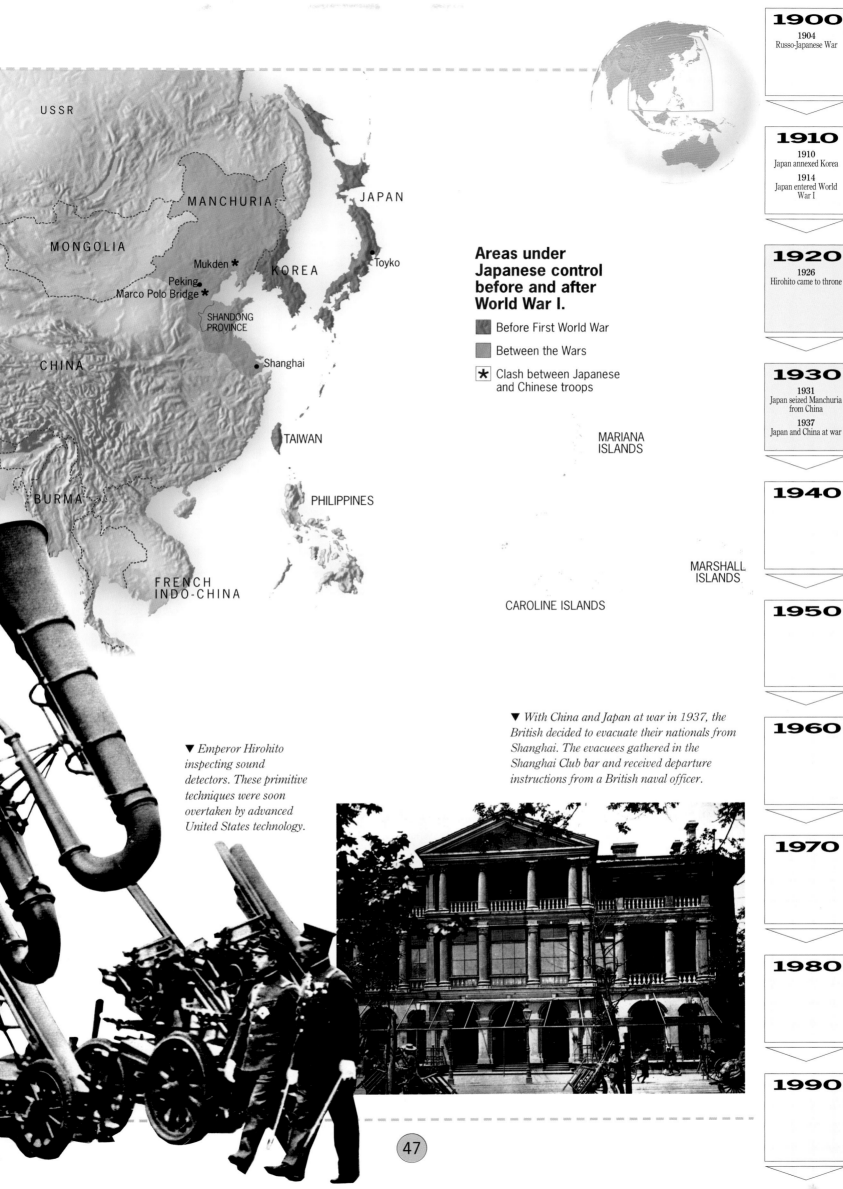

USSR

MONGOLIA

MANCHURIA

JAPAN

Mukden *

KOREA

Toyko

Peking.
Marco Polo Bridge *

SHANDONG
PROVINCE

CHINA

Shanghai

TAIWAN

BURMA

PHILIPPINES

FRENCH
INDO-CHINA

**Areas under
Japanese control
before and after
World War I.**

Before First World War

Between the Wars

* Clash between Japanese
and Chinese troops

MARIANA
ISLANDS

MARSHALL
ISLANDS

CAROLINE ISLANDS

▼ *Emperor Hirohito
inspecting sound
detectors. These primitive
techniques were soon
overtaken by advanced
United States technology.*

▼ *With China and Japan at war in 1937, the
British decided to evacuate their nationals from
Shanghai. The evacuees gathered in the
Shanghai Club bar and received departure
instructions from a British naval officer.*

1900
1904
Russo-Japanese War

1910
1910
Japan annexed Korea
1914
Japan entered World
War I

1920
1926
Hirohito came to throne

1930
1931
Japan seized Manchuria
from China
1937
Japan and China at war

1940

1950

1960

1970

1980

1990

AUSTRALIA AND NEW ZEALAND

DURING THE YEARS BEFORE WORLD WAR I, Australia and New Zealand had begun to throw off some of the political links that tied them to Great Britain. Both nations contributed to the Allied war effort against Germany and Turkey, especially in the Gallipoli campaign (1915–1916) in the Dardanelles. This contribution was recognized at the peace table, when both countries signed the Versailles peace treaty in 1919 and became members of the League of Nations, the new body set up to try to keep world peace.

New dominions

Complete independence from British influence was now demanded. In 1931, Australia and New Zealand, with other countries, including Britain, became partners of equal status in the Commonwealth of Nations. In the 1930s, the mood in some parts of Australia began to run against its links with the British monarchy, but no decisive action was taken.

The depression years of the late 1920s and 1930s hit Australia and New Zealand badly. One in three Australians lost their jobs. Wheat and wool prices fell, which devastated both these farming nations. They had relied on selling their agricultural products worldwide. Now their trade shrank overnight.

▲ These Australian postage stamps commemorate two famous aviators, Charles Ulm and Charles Kingsford-Smith, whose pioneering flights opened up the Australian outback.

▼ In July 1913, King George V laid the foundation stone of Australia House in the Strand, London.

The thirties

In New Zealand the government aimed to boost farming, business, and industry by giving the state a bigger role in the economy. In a land of vast distances like Australia, transport is vital. The 1930s saw experiments with a form of transport that was soon to provide a new lifeline: aircraft.

Australia and New Zealand produced world-class figures in science and the arts. New Zealand-born scientist Ernest Rutherford (1871–1937), working abroad, discovered the atom in 1919. Writers such as New Zealand-born Katherine Mansfield (1888–1923) and Australian Patrick White (1912–90) also became famous for their work.

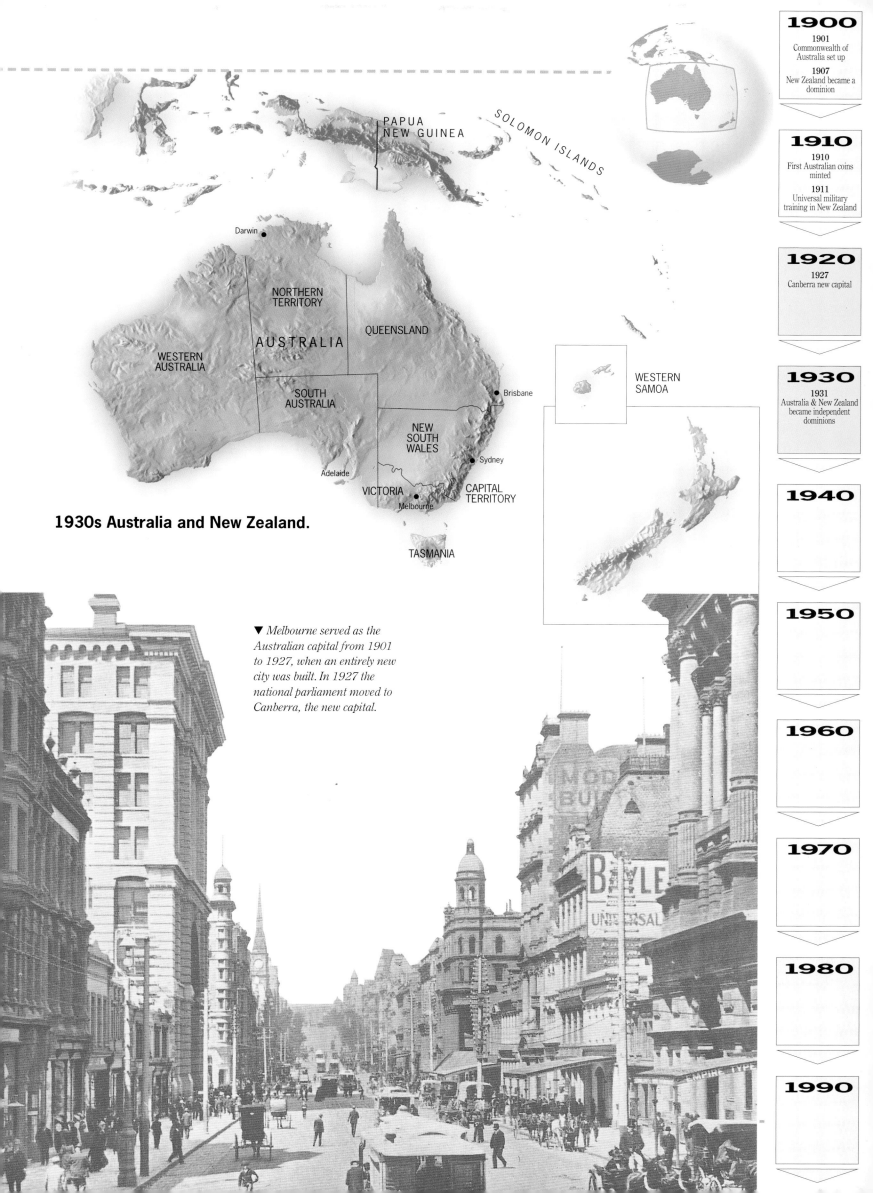

PAPUA
NEW GUINEA

SOLOMON ISLANDS

Darwin

NORTHERN
TERRITORY

AUSTRALIA

WESTERN
AUSTRALIA

QUEENSLAND

SOUTH
AUSTRALIA

Brisbane

WESTERN
SAMOA

NEW
SOUTH
WALES

Sydney

Adelaide

VICTORIA

CAPITAL
TERRITORY

Melbourne

1930s Australia and New Zealand.

TASMANIA

▼ *Melbourne served as the*
Australian capital from 1901
to 1927, when an entirely new
city was built. In 1927 the
national parliament moved to
Canberra, the new capital.

1900
1901
Commonwealth of
Australia set up
1907
New Zealand became a
dominion

1910
1910
First Australian coins
minted
1911
Universal military
training in New Zealand

1920
1927
Canberra new capital

1930
1931
Australia & New Zealand
became independent
dominions

1940

1950

1960

1970

1980

1990

CHINA

REVOLUTION IN CHINA in 1911 overturned rule by the imperial dynasty and a republic was set up. Different factions clashed as independent warlords and army officers struggled for power. Two groups pointed the way ahead: the Nationalists, or Kuomintang (KMT), and the Chinese Communist Party. Based in Canton, Sun Yat-sen of the KMT forged an alliance with the newly-formed Communist Party in 1921. Together they sought to unite their country and to free it from foreign influence. When Sun died in 1925, a big drive took place to try to realize this aim, spearheaded by KMT army officer Chiang Kai-shek (1887–1975).

Civil war

Chiang made enemies of his Communist allies, and civil war broke out between the two in 1927. Communist leader Mao Zedong (1893–1976) organized guerilla opposition to the KMT, and built up support for the Communists among the peasants of the countryside. A major assault on the Communists forced Mao and his supporters to abandon their base in Kiangsi Province and march north. This was the Long March (1934–1935), an epic 5000-mile (8000-km) trek to safety in Yenan.

Lack of industry

China was still largely an agricultural land. Industry was confined to areas under foreign control – Manchuria, which was controlled by the Japanese, and the treaty ports such as Shanghai. Working conditions were basic. Young boy workers in Shanghai suffered from work-related diseases such as lead poisoning and silicosis. In the countryside, too, conditions were grim. Food was in short supply and disease rarely far away.

▲ *Chiang Kai-shek helped form the Kuomintang (Chinese Nationalist Party) in 1918 and became its political and military leader in 1926.*

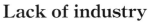

◀ *Mao Zedong (left) in Kiansi province in 1937, two years after The Long March from Kiangsi, which established him as Chinese Communist Party leader.*

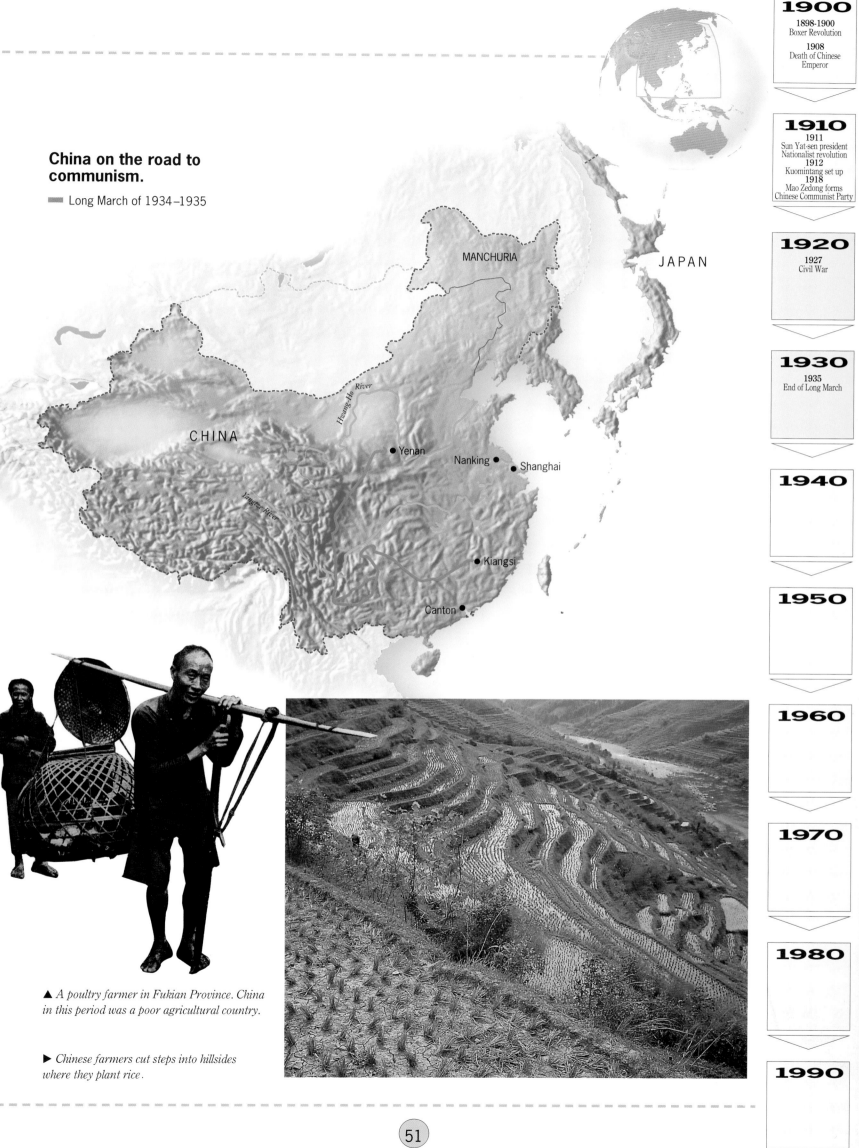

China on the road to communism.

▬▬ Long March of 1934–1935

MANCHURIA

JAPAN

CHINA

Hwang-Ho River

Yenan •

Nanking • • Shanghai

Yangtse River

• Kiangsi

Canton •

▲ *A poultry farmer in Fukian Province. China in this period was a poor agricultural country.*

▶ *Chinese farmers cut steps into hillsides where they plant rice.*

1900
1898-1900
Boxer Revolution
1908
Death of Chinese Emperor

1910
1911
Sun Yat-sen president
Nationalist revolution
1912
Kuomintang set up
1918
Mao Zedong forms
Chinese Communist Party

1920
1927
Civil War

1930
1935
End of Long March

1940

1950

1960

1970

1980

1990

SOUTHERN ASIA

THE NATIONALIST FEELING THAT had begun to grow in India before World War I gained new force after the war. Many Indians were disappointed that peace had not brought them greater freedom. The Indian National Congress gained mass support, thanks to its leader Mohandas Gandhi (1869–1948). Gandhi campaigned for worker and peasant rights, unity between Hindu and Muslim, and for Indian freedom. In Ceylon and Burma, political change was in the air. In the Dutch East Indies and French Indochina, communist movements pushed the cause of independence under radical leaders like Vietnam's Ho Chi Minh (1890–1969).

Nationalist feeling

Peaceful non-cooperation with the British and passive resistance were Gandhi's key tactics. These included hunger strikes and boycotts of British goods. Such protests led to mass arrests. Gandhi himself was put in prison many times. So, too, was Congress member Jawaharlal Nehru (1889–1964), who was later to become India's first prime minister.

▶ *Mohandas Gandhi (1869–1948) the Indian National Congress leader, after the conference in London in 1931.*

British reaction to the rising tide of Indian feeling varied. In the Punjab in 1919 troops opened fire on a crowd in Amritsar, killing 379 people and wounding many others. But thanks to pressure from the National Congress and Muslim League, negotiations between the Indian nationalists and the British government began in the late 1920s. Important acts of parliament in Britain paved the way for Indian independence. Government of India Acts in 1919 and 1935 set up the machinery for India to rule itself.

A Muslim homeland

However, religious differences between the Hindus and Muslims began to split Indian society. Congress was mainly Hindu. The Muslim leader Mohammed Ali Jinnah (1876–1948) sought Hindu-Muslim cooperation when bloody riots broke out, and argued for a separate homeland for the Muslims.

◀ *British India faced Muslim–Hindu strife as well as anti-British unrest. Here, British troops guard a temple after riots in Calcutta.*

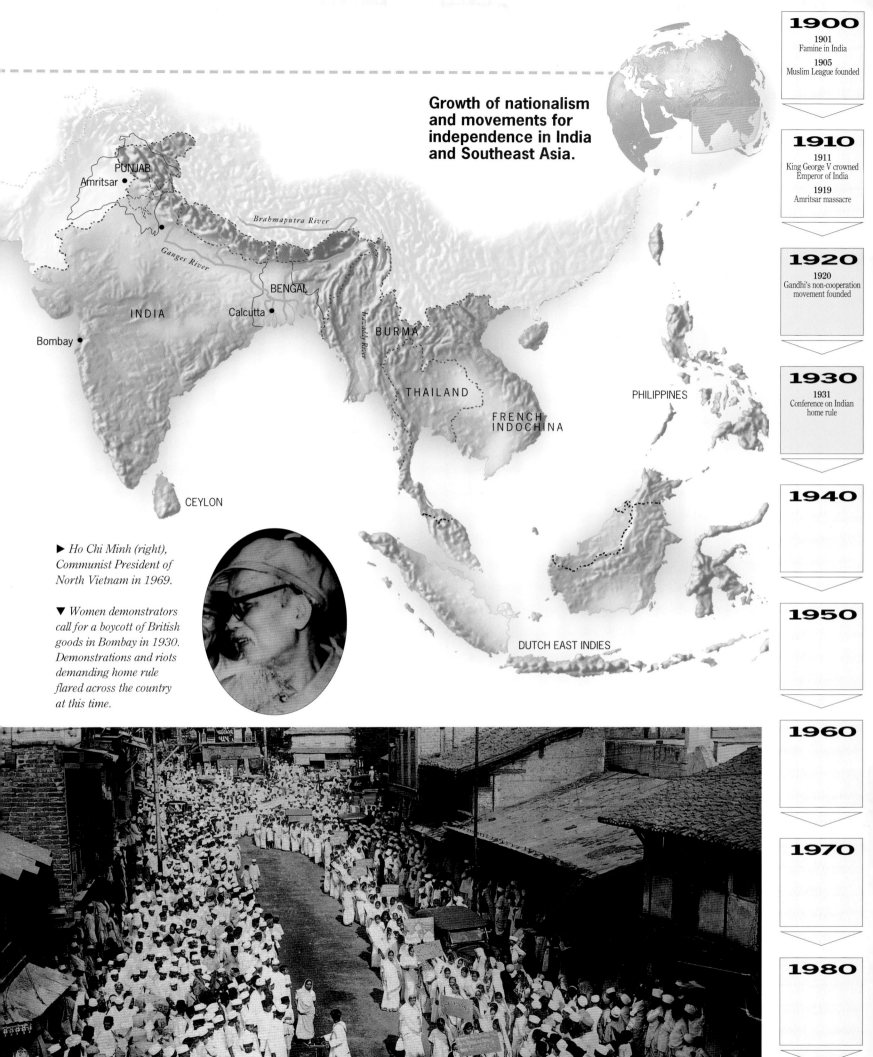

Growth of nationalism and movements for independence in India and Southeast Asia.

PUNJAB
Amritsar •

Brahmaputra River

Ganges River

BENGAL

INDIA

Calcutta •

Bombay •

Irrawaddy River

BURMA

THAILAND

FRENCH INDOCHINA

PHILIPPINES

CEYLON

DUTCH EAST INDIES

▶ *Ho Chi Minh (right), Communist President of North Vietnam in 1969.*

▼ *Women demonstrators call for a boycott of British goods in Bombay in 1930. Demonstrations and riots demanding home rule flared across the country at this time.*

1900
1901
Famine in India
1905
Muslim League founded

1910
1911
King George V crowned
Emperor of India
1919
Amritsar massacre

1920
1920
Gandhi's non-cooperation
movement founded

1930
1931
Conference on Indian
home rule

1940

1950

1960

1970

1980

1990

AFRICA

THE POLITICAL SHAKE-UP caused by World War I was felt by many African countries. Germany's empire was dismantled and divided up between the victors. South Africa received South West Africa; Belgium took Rwanda-Urundi. Britain and France shared the Cameroons and Togo. Britain took Tanganyika. Like other colonies redistributed after the War, these were "mandates," ruled under the watchful eye of the League of Nations, with the idea that one day they might become independent.

African trade

Economics put many parts of Africa at a disadvantage, as the colonial powers exploited Africa's great potential.

Portugal promoted cotton growing in its African colonies. Gold and diamonds came out of South Africa's mines. These enriched European countries and white settlers in Africa, and only rarely the Africans themselves.

▲ From a country whose wealth depended on farming, South Africa became an industrial country. Johannesburg became one of Africa's largest cities.

◄ The way that colonial powers interfered in Africa was shown when Italian troops invaded Abyssinia in 1935–36. Here Abyssinian troops parade before their ruler, Emperor Haile Selassie, in 1935.

The Gold Coast was an exception. Here, cocoa farming was introduced in the 1890s, and although most of the profits went to European trading companies, some Africans benefitted, too.

Rise of nationalism

When recession hit the developed world, this affected Africa as prices for exports like cocoa fell dramatically. Economic grievances helped boost support for new nationalist leaders like Nnandi Azikiwe (b.1904). Azikiwe set up a newspaper on the Gold Coast that voiced nationalist ideas and reached many people. When Nigeria gained independence, Azikiwe became its first president in 1963.

◄ Discontentment with traditional lifestyles led some Africans to leave the countryside, hoping for better conditions in the towns.

▲ *In Portuguese colonies cotton was grown for sale overseas. Often there was not enough land to grow food.*

▼ *Africa's Gold Coast was named for its gold and diamonds. In the colonial period, these were exploited by Europeans using black labor.*

Mandates in Africa under the League of Nations.

- France and Britain
- Great Britain
- Belgium
- South Africa
- Invaded by Italy 1935

GOLD COAST TOGO
NIGERIA
CAMEROONS
ABYSSINIA
RUANDA-URUNDI
TANGANYIKA
SOUTH WEST AFRICA
Johannesburg
SOUTH AFRICA

1900
1902
End of Boer War
1904
French West Africa created

1910
1912
ANC formed
1917
Haile Selassie becomes Emperor of Ethiopia

1920
1922
Egypt gains independence

1930
1935
Mussolini invades Ethiopia

1940

1950

1960

1970

1980

1990

THE MIDDLE EAST

WORLD WAR I RESHAPED the map of the Middle East. The Ottoman Empire collapsed, leaving Britain and France eagerly picking up the pieces. France received Syria and Lebanon as League of Nation mandates. Britain took Iraq, Jordan, and Palestine. In 1923 the Republic of Turkey was also created out of the skeleton of the Ottoman Empire. All that remained of the former Ottoman Empire were Constantinople (renamed Istanbul) and Asia Minor.

A Jewish homeland

Britain and France had encouraged Arab nationalists during the war and when peace failed to give independence, tension mounted. There was Arab unease, too, about British support in 1917 for a homeland for the Jews in Palestine. Known as the Balfour Declaration, this statement antagonized Arabs. Jewish settlement in Palestine increased and kibbutzim (cooperative farms) were set up, but Jewish settlers were met with hostility and violence.

▲ *Cooperative farms known as kibbutzim were set up in Israel from the turn of the century.*

New Arab states

Britain had become the leading power in the Middle East, but it met challenge, especially from Egypt, and powers of self-government were gradually delivered. Iraq became independent in 1930, for example, and Saudi Arabia was established as a kingdom in 1932.

New nationalist governments came to power in other parts of the Middle East. Mustafa Kemal, known as Ataturk, or Father of the Turks (1881–1938), led Turkey toward a more modern future, encouraging women's liberation and refusing to allow Islam to influence his policies. In Iran, an army coup in 1926 brought Reza Shah Pahlavi (1878–1944) to power. Middle East society blended ancient, especially Islamic, and modern ways of life. The story of oil-rich Saudi Arabia shows the process of change.

◄ *Increasing numbers of Jewish settlers, like those shown here, arrived in Palestine after World War I. This alarmed the local Arab population and led to conflict.*

Constantinople

TURKEY
1923

ASIA MINOR

Caspian Sea

Mediterranean Sea

SYRIA

LEBANON

IRAQ
gained
independence
1930

PALESTINE

TRANS-JORDAN

IRAN
(formerly Persia)

The Gulf

AFRICA

Red Sea

SAUDI ARABIA
became kingdom
1932

**Mandates in the
Middle East under the
League of Nations.**

☐ France
☐ Britain

YEMEN
1930

1900
1902
Ibn Saud captures
Riyadh, Saudi Arabia
1908
Pan-Islamic movement
begins in Turkey

1910
1917
Balfour Declaration

1920
1923
Republic of Turkey
created

1930
1930
Iraq gains independence
1932
Saudi Arabia established

1940

1950

1960

1970

1980

1990

◄ *This monument is to
Mustafa Kemal,
remembered as Ataturk,
father of the Turks.
Ataturk ruled as a
dictator, and was
responsible for many
social reforms.*

▲ *Ataturk wanted to
divorce religion from
politics in Turkey. He
encouraged the use of
surnames, a Western
practice, believing that
Western ways had
something to teach his
country.*

THE WAY OF THE WORLD

The power of economics was felt all over the world in the years between World War I (1914–1918) and World War II (1939–1945). The American stockmarket crash in 1929 led to worldwide recession and the Great Depression. Industrialized countries suffered soaring unemployment, and collapsing banks and businesses. Countries in Asia, Africa, and South America that relied on selling raw materials and foods to world markets had to stand by and watch as falling prices hit crops like coffee, bananas, and rubber.

The recovery

In the middle of the 1930s the world gradually began to claw its way to recovery. The world divided into roughly five areas for trade: one dominated by the U.S. and the dollar; one by Great Britain and the pound; one by Japan and the yen; one by Germany and the mark; and one that stressed the importance of gold in world trade. New York took over from London as an important financial center.

In the West, recovery from depression meant a rise in living standards. New consumer goods like refrigerators and washing machines appeared. The advertising industry developed as manufacturers looked for new ways of persuading people to buy their goods. Science and technology sparked constant change. Radio developed in the 1920s, and television in the 1930s. Technology also took to the skies as new air routes opened.

▶ By the 1930s the Hollywood film industry dominated world theaters. The famous film comedians Laurel and Hardy (Stan Laurel and Oliver Hardy) appeared in many highly-acclaimed films of the period.

CANADA $

UNITED STATES $

$

SOUTH AMERICA

M

£

ARGENTINA

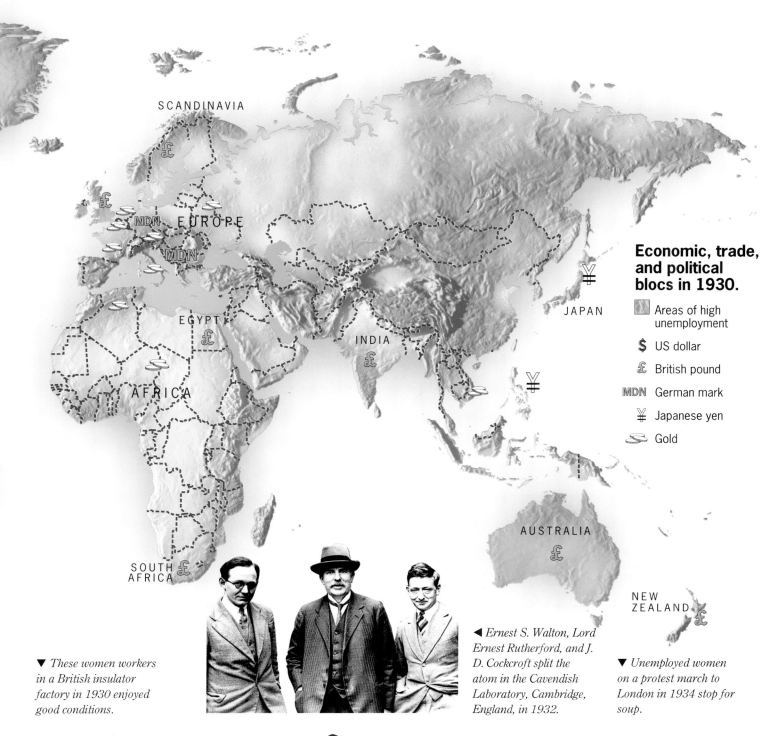

SCANDINAVIA

EUROPE

EGYPT

AFRICA

SOUTH
AFRICA

JAPAN

INDIA

AUSTRALIA

NEW
ZEALAND

**Economic, trade,
and political
blocs in 1930.**

Areas of high
unemployment

$ US dollar

£ British pound

MDN German mark

¥ Japanese yen

Gold

◀ *Ernest S. Walton, Lord
Ernest Rutherford, and J.
D. Cockcroft split the
atom in the Cavendish
Laboratory, Cambridge,
England, in 1932.*

▼ *These women workers
in a British insulator
factory in 1930 enjoyed
good conditions.*

▼ *Unemployed women
on a protest march to
London in 1934 stop for
soup.*

WORLD WAR II: CAUSES

THE WORLD ECONOMIC SLUMP OF 1929–1934 brought important political change around the globe. In Asia, Africa, and Latin America, economies depended on supplying world customers with food and raw materials. Here, economic hardship triggered a surge of support for new, more extreme nationalist leaders, such as Jawaharlal Nehru (1889–1964) in India and Ho Chi Minh (1890–1969) in Vietnam.

The rise of dictators

Among industrialized nations, politics divided into two opposing camps. Some, like the U.S., championed democracy. Others looked for strong leadership at almost any cost. In these countries, dictators came to power: Adolf Hitler (1889–1945) in Germany; Benito Mussolini (1883–1945) in Italy; General Francisco Franco (1892–1975) in Spain; Joseph Stalin (1879–1953) in the Soviet Union. The strong rule developed by right-wing dictators like Mussolini was known as fascism. In the Soviet Union, on the other hand, the government was dedicated to left-wing communism.

▲ *Juan Péron (1895–1974) held power in Argentina after World War II.*

German militarization

In Europe, German resentment of the Treaty of Versailles was an important factor. Hitler won support by promising to re-establish German power. The army was rebuilt, and in 1936 troops were sent into the demilitarized Rhineland. Germany expanded into Austria and Czechoslovakia. The final trigger to European war came in 1939, when Germany invaded Poland. France and Britain then declared war on Germany.

▲ *General Franco became dictator of Spain in 1939, after three years of bitter civil war. Soon he was to ban all political opposition.*

▶ *Nazi supporters believed in right-wing politics and were opposed to communist ideas. They championed the idea that the Germans were a "master race," destined to rule Europe.*

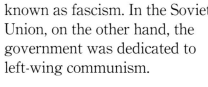

CANADA

UNITED STATES

ESTONIA
LATVIA
LITHUANIA
GREAT
BRITAIN
USSR
GERMANY
AUSTRIA **1938**
POLAND **1939**
CZECHOSLOVAKIA **1938** and **1939**
ROMANIA
YUGOSLAVIA
PORTUGAL SPAIN
ITALY GREECE
TURKEY
CHINA
JAPAN
INDIA
AFRICA
SOUTH
AMERICA
ARGENTINA

HAWAIIAN
ISLANDS (U.S.)

Pearl Harbor

The rise of fascism and communism in the 1930s.

1938 German expansion

Countries with dictators

Countries with strong central rule

Pearl Harbor

In December 1941 a Japanese attack on the U.S. naval base at Pearl Harbor in Hawaii brought the United States into the War. Eight battleships were damaged in the attack, and 177 aircraft were destroyed.

WORLD WAR II: LEADERS

◄ *Charles de Gaulle rallied the Free French from London during World War II.*

IN GERMANY, war was masterminded by "Der Führer" (the leader), Adolf Hitler. He believed that the Germans were a master race, and that it was their right to expand into other areas of Europe. Fanatical and obsessive racist ideas also made him violently anti-Semitic (opposed to the Jews).

▼ *Jewish children wash the streets in Poland on the orders of Nazi leaders.*

The Axis Powers and Russia

Hitler's main allies, Italy and Japan, were known as the Axis Powers. Italy was led by Benito Mussolini. Japan fought under Emperor Hirohito. Japan's war aims included linking Asia closely to the Japanese economy. Joseph Stalin directed Russia's war. At the beginning of the war, Russia had reached an understanding with Germany. But in 1941, Hitler attacked Russia. Joining the Allies, Russia fought back powerfully.

The Allies

The main Allied powers were Britain, France, and from 1941, the U.S. After 1940 Britain was led by Prime Minister Winston Churchill (1874–1965). America had given the Allies some material support early in the war, but many people felt it was not America's quarrel. The Japanese attack on Pearl Harbor in 1941 changed this, and America came into the war under President F. D. Roosevelt (1882–1945). After the fall of France in 1940, French resistance to Germany was led by Charles de Gaulle (1890–1970).

▲ *Japanese Admiral Isoroku Yamamoto (1884–1943) played a crucial part in building up the Japanese navy.*

► *Hitler aimed to overthrow the peace settlement that had been established after World War I and build up a position of German superiority.*

◄ *Churchill gives a "V for Victory" salute at 10, Downing street.*

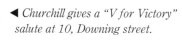

CANADA

UNITED STATES

MEXICO

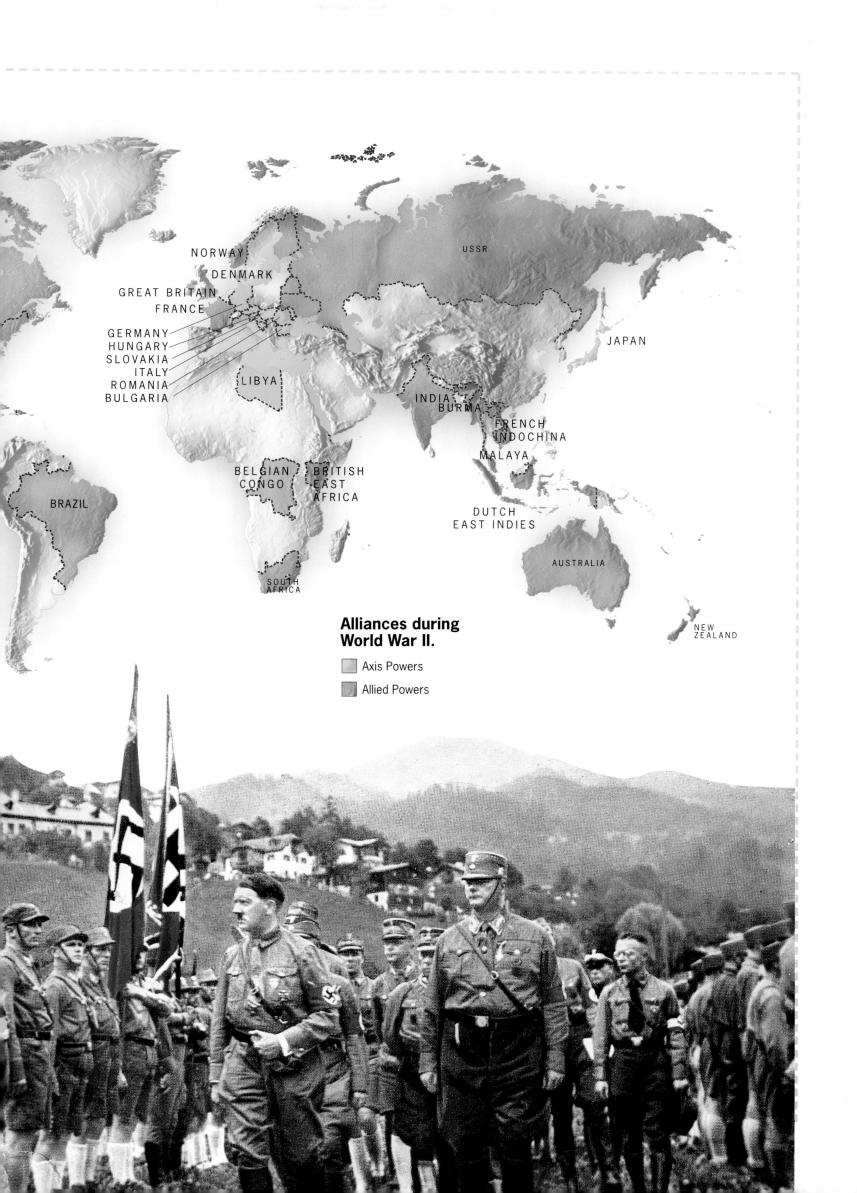

NORWAY

DENMARK

GREAT BRITAIN

FRANCE

GERMANY
HUNGARY
SLOVAKIA
ITALY
ROMANIA
BULGARIA

USSR

JAPAN

LIBYA

INDIA
BURMA

FRENCH
INDOCHINA

MALAYA

BELGIAN
CONGO

BRITISH
EAST
AFRICA

DUTCH
EAST INDIES

BRAZIL

SOUTH
AFRICA

AUSTRALIA

NEW
ZEALAND

**Alliances during
World War II.**

Axis Powers

Allied Powers

WORLD WAR II: ARMIES

WAR IN EUROPE BEGAN with a series of rapid attacks by Germany. Tanks and motorized armed vehicles, backed up by dive bombers, rolled relentlessly across Europe. Norway, Denmark, Belgium, the Netherlands, and France fell to Hitler's armies in 1940. This lightning war was known as Blitzkrieg. Now only Britain stood against Germany in Europe. Hitler hoped to invade, paving the way with an air attack that became known as the Battle of Britain. Science came to the aid of the British war effort when radar was used for the first time to pinpoint enemy planes. A large number of German bombers were shot down and Hitler abandoned his invasion plans.

The war in Europe

Fighting spread as Italy attacked Greece and Egypt. In 1941 German armies were sent against Russia. Russian armies fought back energetically and forced a German retreat by 1943. The Russian campaign is known in Russia as the Great Patriotic War. Millions of Russians lost their lives defending their homeland. Failure in Russia began to turn the tide against Germany. America entered the war in 1941. Italy surrendered to the Allies in 1943, and in 1944 there were the D Day landings in Normandy, when the Allies invaded France. Germany, squeezed by Allied offensives from both east and west, surrendered in May 1945.

The war in the East

War in the East lasted longer than war in Europe. In 1941 the Japanese bombed the US naval base at Pearl Harbor, which brought America into the war. In 1945 Japan surrendered after atomic bombs were dropped on the two Japanese cities of Hiroshima and Nagasaki.

CANADA

UNITED STATES

▲ *British and French troops were forced to retreat to Dunkirk in 1940 and a heroic rescue bid was staged. These soldiers are struggling to reach a waiting ship.*

◀ *These men were among the first American troops to go into action in Asia. Here, they advance into Northern Burma to put pressure on the Japanese.*

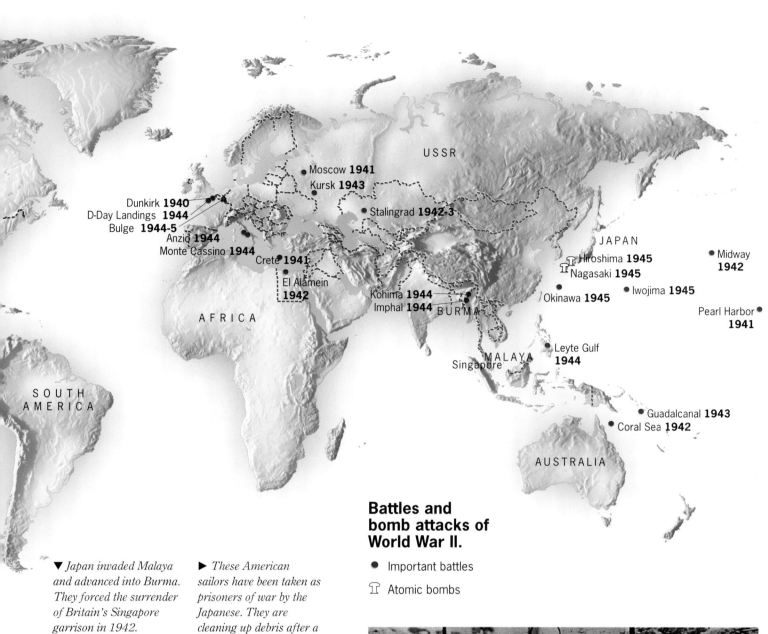

Moscow **1941**
Kursk **1943**
Stalingrad **1942-3**
Dunkirk **1940**
D-Day Landings **1944**
Bulge **1944-5**
Anzio **1944**
Monte Cassino **1944**
Crete **1941**
El Alamein **1942**
Kohima **1944**
Imphal **1944**
BURMA
Hiroshima **1945**
Nagasaki **1945**
Midway **1942**
Iwojima **1945**
Okinawa **1945**
Pearl Harbor **1941**
Leyte Gulf **1944**
Singapore
MALAYA
Guadalcanal **1943**
Coral Sea **1942**

USSR
JAPAN
AFRICA
SOUTH AMERICA
AUSTRALIA

Battles and bomb attacks of World War II.

● Important battles

♆ Atomic bombs

▼ *Japan invaded Malaya and advanced into Burma. They forced the surrender of Britain's Singapore garrison in 1942.*

▶ *These American sailors have been taken as prisoners of war by the Japanese. They are cleaning up debris after a bomb attack.*

WORLD WAR II: CIVILIANS

WORLD WAR II was waged on a greater scale than any previous war, and it affected ordinary people as well as soldiers. With the men away at war, there was a shortage of workers. Germany used prisoners of war, Jews, and others held in concentration camps, and people from occupied countries as slave labor. Japan brought in labor from other countries, such as Korea. In America, large numbers of women worked in munitions and aircraft factories.

Indiscriminate bombing

Civilians became targets of war in bombing raids. Britain and Germany bombed each other's cities. Japan bombed targets in China. In countries like Britain and Japan children were evacuated from the cities and sent to the countryside to be safe. Pressure on food supplies led to severe rationing.

War crimes

Terrible atrocities were carried out by Germany and Japan against people in land they occupied. Nazi Germany aimed to destroy the Jewish people. Death camps were set up as part of this policy, and by 1945 over six million Jews had been killed.

▼ *Large numbers of civilians in Britain became involved in the war effort dealing with the results of air raids.*

▲ *On the outbreak of war in September 1939, thousands of London schoolchildren were evacuated to escape German bombing. Here a soldier on leave says goodbye to his son.*

▶ *A Canadian tank assembly plant in 1942. This Montreal Company was a United States subsidiary. Munitions and weapons production in North America expanded dramatically after 1941.*

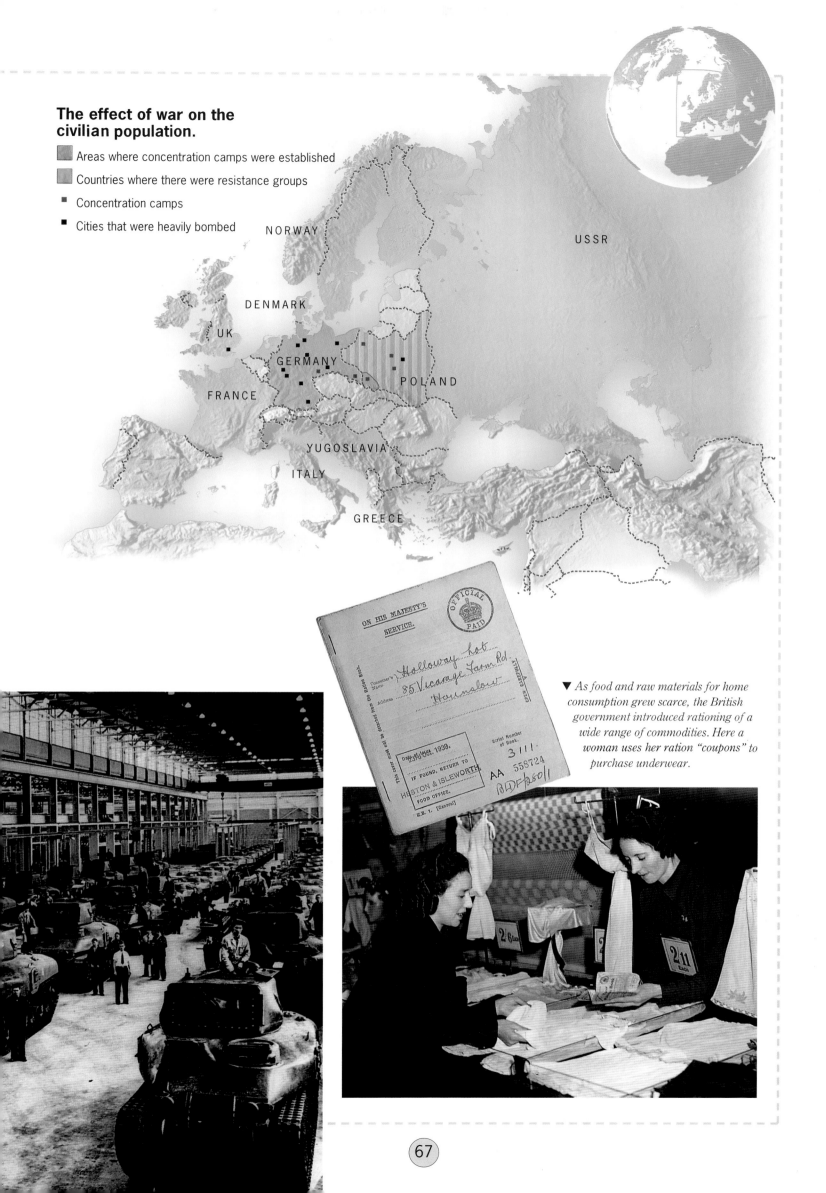

The effect of war on the civilian population.

- Areas where concentration camps were established
- Countries where there were resistance groups
- Concentration camps
- Cities that were heavily bombed

NORWAY

USSR

DENMARK

UK

GERMANY

POLAND

FRANCE

YUGOSLAVIA

ITALY

GREECE

▼ *As food and raw materials for home consumption grew scarce, the British government introduced rationing of a wide range of commodities. Here a woman uses her ration "coupons" to purchase underwear.*

COLD WAR

Out of the war a new power balance was born. The United States and the Soviet Union became dominant world powers, or super powers, each with the capacity to make nuclear weapons. Talks held at Yalta and Potsdam in 1945 were dominated by the "Big Three" – the U.S. under Roosevelt, Britain under Churchill, and the USSR under Stalin. Germany was divided into four zones (with France) each occupied and ruled by the Allied Powers. In 1949 these zones were merged into two, creating the Federal Republic of Germany in the West, and the Russian-influenced German Democratic Republic in the East. The city of Berlin was also divided between East and West.

▲ *In 1945 Stalin, Roosevelt, and Churchill met at Yalta in the Soviet Union to discuss plans for the last stages of World War II.*

The new divisions

America feared that Russia was planning a worldwide communist takeover. Russia feared that democratic, capitalist America and its allies threatened Russian existence. Each side built up influence in other countries to counter this perceived threat. This, so people said at the time, was different from the heat of nuclear war. It was "cold war".

Cold War began in Europe, as Russia began to build up a network of allies in the countries on its borders. By 1948, communist governments had been set up in many countries of eastern Europe, including Hungary, Poland, Bulgaria, and Czechoslovakia. Cold War spread, around the globe. In Asia, Russia and the Allies supported opposing sides in the Korean War of 1950–1953. In Cuba, a build-up of Russian missiles threatened nuclear war in 1962.

▲ *Wartime bombing left a trail of chaos and destruction in many German cities. Here, the women of Dresden help to rebuild their city after the war.*

▲ *Although conflict on a global scale has been avoided since World War II, there have been many devastating regional wars. The Korean War was one of these.*

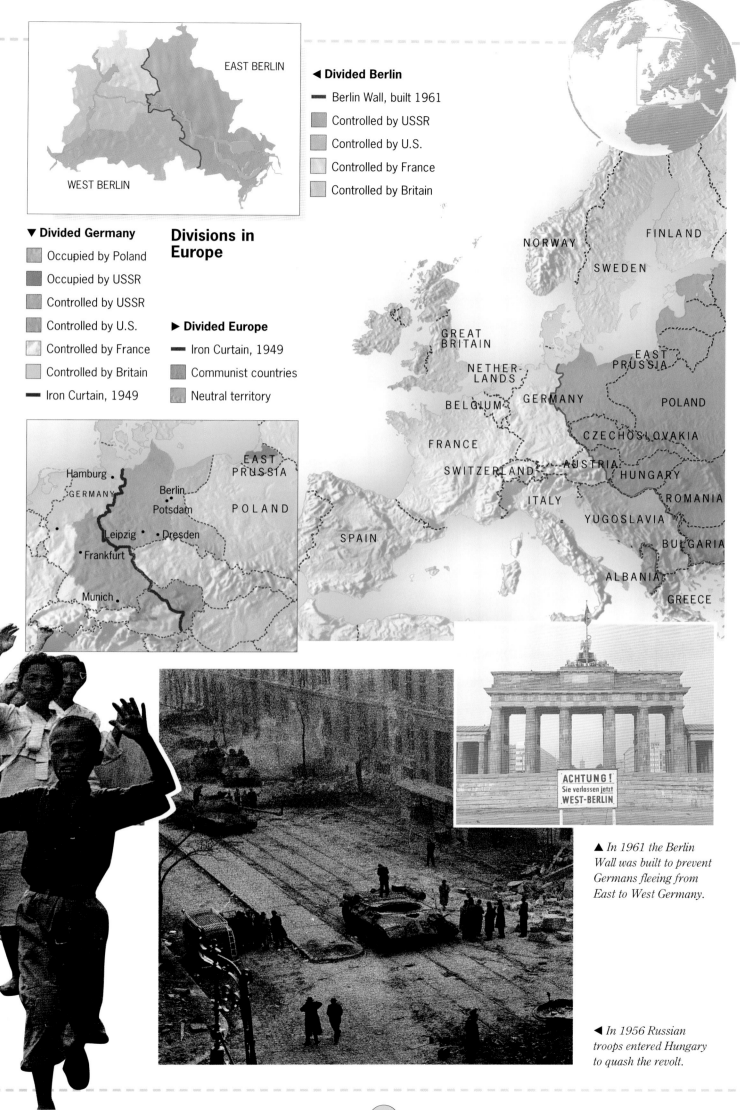

EAST BERLIN

WEST BERLIN

◄ Divided Berlin

— Berlin Wall, built 1961

Controlled by USSR

Controlled by U.S.

Controlled by France

Controlled by Britain

▼ Divided Germany

Occupied by Poland

Occupied by USSR

Controlled by USSR

Controlled by U.S.

Controlled by France

Controlled by Britain

— Iron Curtain, 1949

Divisions in Europe

► Divided Europe

— Iron Curtain, 1949

Communist countries

Neutral territory

Hamburg
GERMANY
EAST PRUSSIA
Berlin
Potsdam
POLAND
Leipzig • Dresden
Frankfurt
Munich

NORWAY
FINLAND
SWEDEN
GREAT BRITAIN
NETHER-LANDS
EAST PRUSSIA
BELGIUM
GERMANY
POLAND
FRANCE
CZECHOSLOVAKIA
SWITZERLAND
AUSTRIA
HUNGARY
ITALY
ROMANIA
SPAIN
YUGOSLAVIA
BULGARIA
ALBANIA
GREECE

ACHTUNG!
Sie verlassen jetzt
WEST-BERLIN

▲ *In 1961 the Berlin Wall was built to prevent Germans fleeing from East to West Germany.*

◄ *In 1956 Russian troops entered Hungary to quash the revolt.*

U.S. AND CANADA

THE AMERICAN ECONOMY STARTED to boom in the 1940s. After the war, consumer demand increased as a result of population growth. Many people moved from the countryside to fast-growing towns and even faster-growing suburbs. The area between Boston and Washington was nicknamed "Megalopolis," or Giant City, as the suburbs spread in the 1960s. The American West thrived as more people moved to states like California. Prosperity has since shifted from old manufacturing cities like Detroit in the north, to service centers in the south, such as Phoenix, Arizona. Interstate highways were built to link different parts of the country. Until the world oil crisis of 1973, fuel was cheap. Cars rolled off the production line and housing was easily affordable.

▲ *Dwight D. Eisenhower was elected U.S. President in 1952. The photograph shows his inauguration parade in 1953.*

Civil rights

In the 1950s and 1960s, it became obvious that one part of the population was not sharing America's prosperity or its political freedom. The civil rights movement led by Martin Luther King Jr.(1929–1968) sponsored black equality. The 1960s seemed a time of high political ideals. King's peaceful protests for Black rights captured world imagination; so, too, did President John F. Kennedy (1917–1963). "Ask not what your country can do for you – ask what you can do for your country," Kennedy demanded. New social programs were put forward by President Lyndon B. Johnson (1908–1973).

In Canada

The 1960s saw a movement to turn Quebec into a separate French-speaking state. Newfoundland was joined to Canada constitutionally in 1949. Population and industry expanded, with resources such as iron ore and uranium bringing greater prosperity.

▲ *John F. Kennedy was assassinated in Dallas, Texas, in 1963. His short-lived presidency was heralded with much fanfare.*

Economic growth and social change in North America after World War II.

![Population movement] Population movement

○ Areas of economic growth

□ Key places in civil rights movements

ALASKA

CANADA

UNITED STATES

NEWFOUNDLAND

ONTARIO

Quebec
Ottawa

Seattle

IDAHO
NEVADA

MASSACHUSETTS
Boston

New York
PENNSYLVANIA

CALIFORNIA

Chicago
Detroit
OHIO

Washington D.C.
VIRGINIA

Kansas City

NORTH CAROLINA

Los Angeles

MISSOURI

Greensboro

ARKANSAS
Memphis

ARIZONA
Little Rock

Phoenix

Birmingham
Montgomery
Selma
ALABAMA

Atlanta

GEORGIA

Dallas

Houston
LOUISIANA

▲ *A successful motion picture and cartoon business, Disney has recently expanded into theme parks.*

▼ *Martin Luther King, Jr. (1929–1968), an outstanding Afro-American civil rights leader and orator, was assassinated in Memphis, Tennessee, in 1968.*

▼ *In 1957 Arkansas Governor Orval Faubus sent national guardsmen to prevent black students entering Central High School, Little Rock.*

1900
1901-9
T. Roosevelt president
1903
First powered flight

1910
1912
Arizona and New Mexico US states
1919
Prohibition begins

1920
1929
Wall Street Crash

1930
1932
F.D. Roosevelt elected president
1933
Tennessee Valley Authority

1940
1941
U.S. enters WW2

1950
1952
Eva Peron died
1957
Race riots, Arkansas

1960
1961
Kennedy elected president
1963
Kennedy assassinated
1968
King assassinated
1969
Nixon president

1970
1972
Congress passes Equal Opportunities Act
1974
Watergate scandal

1980
1980
Reagan wins for Republicans
1989
U.S. troops invade Panama

1990
1990
U.S. bombs Iraqi missile sites

SOUTH AMERICA

DEPRESSION IN THE 1930s, followed by World War II, cut South America off from markets overseas. Some countries looked for new areas to branch into and Argentina, under President Juan Domingo Peron (1895–1974), made swift industrial growth. Governments in Guatemala (1944), Bolivia (1952), Cuba (1959), and Chile (1970) promoted socialist policies, nationalizing industry and giving land to the peasants.

Military dictatorship

In many countries the army came to play a strong role in politics, and violence was never far away. In Chile, a military coup ended the elected government of President Salvador Allende (1908–1973) and brought brutal military rule under President Augusto Pinochet (b.1915).

Political instability was also caused by the involvement of external powers. Cuba, under the Marxist government of Fidel Castro (b.1927), was keen to promote revolution throughout South America. Revolutionary leader Che Guevara (1928–1967) helped to launch guerilla movements in Bolivia and other countries as part of this campaign.

The U.S. had also been engaged in Latin American politics, siding especially with those opposed to communist-style rule.

▲ Brasilia was designated the new capital of Brazil in 1960. The spectacular cathedral was designed by architect Oscar Niemeyer.

Foreign debts

During the 1970s, many new industries were set up. Cities grew as country people arrived searching for work and food. To fund industry, governments borrowed from banks around the world.

Repaying foreign debt in the 1980s caused problems for Mexico, Brazil, and other countries and the search for new economic opportunities has led to clearance of the Amazonian rainforest in Surinam and Brazil, and cocaine-manufacturing on a large scale in Bolivia.

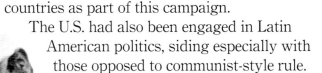

◄ U.S.-backed anti-Marxist guerillas, or Contras, test their American weapons.

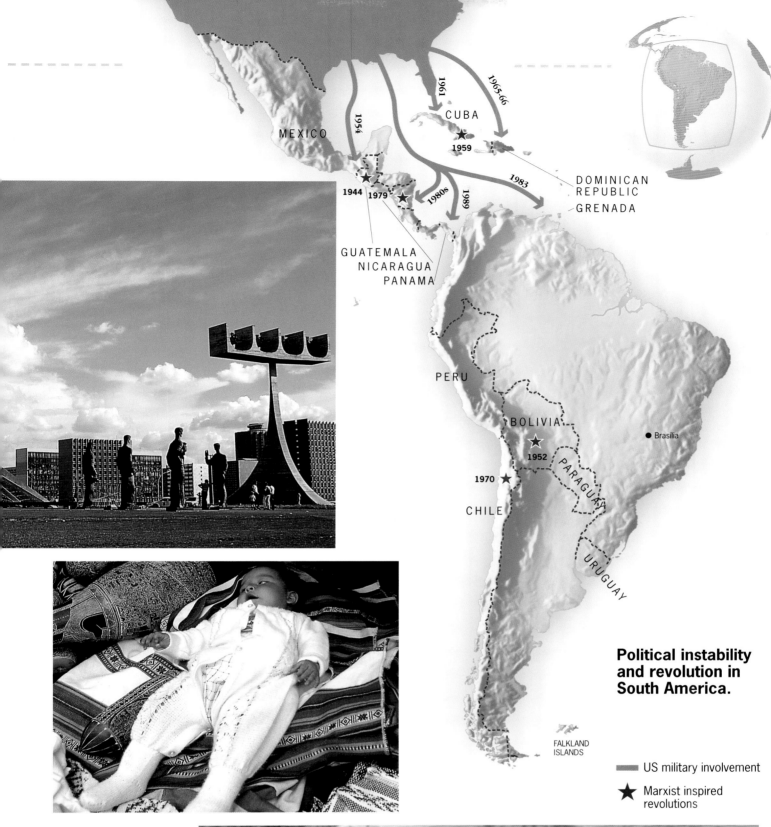

MEXICO

1954

1944 1979

1961

1965-66

CUBA

1959

1983

1980s 1989

DOMINICAN
REPUBLIC
GRENADA

GUATEMALA
NICARAGUA
PANAMA

PERU

BOLIVIA

1952

1970

CHILE

PARAGUAY

Brasilia

URUGUAY

**Political instability
and revolution in
South America.**

FALKLAND
ISLANDS

▬▬▬ US military involvement

★ Marxist inspired
revolutions

▲ *This baby is lying on
traditional hand-woven
cloths. The population of
Peru is of Indian and
European origins.
Fishing, agriculture, and
minerals are its main
resources.*

▶ *A farmer in northern
Brazil helps to destroy the
tropical rainforest by fire.
Scientists fear the effects
on the global climate of
the destruction of the
rainforests.*

1900
1903
Panama secedes from
Colombia
1904-11
Ismael Montez president
of Bolivia

1910
1911
Mexican Revolution
1914
Panama Canal completed

1920
1929
National Revolutionary
Party formed in Mexico

1930
1934-45
Vargas president of Brazil
1934-40
Cárdenas president of
Mexico
1932-5
Chaco War

1940
1943
Chile backs U.S. in World
War I
1946
Juan Peron president of
Argentina

1950
1955
Argentine army seizes
power from President
Perón

1960
1962
Cuban missile crisis

1970
1973
Military coup in Chile
1979
Sandinistas sieze power
in Nicaragua

1980
1980-82
Civil war in El Salvador
1989
US invades Panama

1990
1990
Sandinistas defeated in
Nicaragua

WESTERN EUROPE

WORLD WAR II left western Europe totally exhausted and facing a huge challenge. Bomb destruction had to be repaired, businesses needed to be revived, and millions of refugees and prisoners of war had to be provided with food and shelter. In 1948 aid from America, under the Marshall Plan, paved the way for European recovery.

Trade and industry gradually revived and throughout western Europe the standard of living rose. Wages increased and greater welfare provision was made for workers, the sick, the unemployed, and the elderly. Ordinary working people had more money in their pockets than any other generation.

▲ Margaret Thatcher dominated politics in Britain from 1979–90. Some of her plans involved cutting spending on welfare and privatizing industry.

▼ The Concorde first took to the skies in 1969. The project showed a desire for cooperation between France and Britain.

International organizations

The U.S. and Western European countries set up a defense body, the North Atlantic Treaty Organization (NATO), in 1949. The European Economic Community (now the European Union) was set up in 1958. The United Nations (UN), a new international body set up after the war, speaks on world politics and carries out social programs through bodies such as UNESCO and the World Health Organization (WHO).

▶ Unrest in Cyprus in the 1960s led to the arrival of a United Nations peacekeeping force in l964.

◀ The Channel Tunnel represents a move to draw the people of Europe closer together.

Countries belonging to the European Community.

1973 Date of joining EC

FINLAND
1995

SWEDEN
1995

IRELAND
1973

GREAT
BRITAIN
1973

DENMARK
1973

NETHER-
LANDS
1958

BELGIUM
1958

GERMAN
FEDERAL
REPUBLIC
1958

LUXEMBOURG
1958

AUSTRIA
1995

FRANCE
1958

PORTUGAL
1986

SPAIN
1986

ITALY
1958

GREECE
1981

The Beatles

In the 1960s, pop music was revolutionized by groups such as The Beatles, shown here, and the Rolling Stones. Pop music became part of teenage life and put the swing into the "Swinging Sixties."

1900
1901
Queen Victoria died
1901
First transatlantic radio signal

1910
1910
Monarchy ends in Portugal
1916
Easter Rising

1920
1926
General Strike

1930
1933
Hitler took power
1936
Civil War in Spain

1940
1949
NATO set up

1950
1958
EEC set up

1960
1968
Students riot in Paris

1970
1972
Munich Olympics massacre

1980
1989
Berlin Wall torn down

1990
1990
Reunification of Germany

THE FORMER SOVIET UNION AND EASTERN EUROPE

IN THE FALL OF 1989 TELEVISION SETS screened pictures from Berlin that stunned the world: the Berlin Wall, that divided the city into east and west and marked the boundary between socialist and democratic worlds, was being taken down. Borders inside Eastern Europe were being opened and thousands of jubilant Germans crossed from East to West – the route forbidden for years. Communist governments fell from power in East Germany, Czechoslovakia, Poland, and Romania.

The Soviet Union collapses

The eyes of the world were also on the Soviet Union. What would its reaction be to these astonishing events? In the past, moves for independence in the countries of eastern Europe had been severely repressed. But here, too, there was revolutionary change. The new Soviet leader, Mikhail Gorbachev, who had come to power in 1985, was also talking of the need for change. Under Gorbachev, the Communist Party began to lose its all-powerful position in Soviet politics. There was a new willingness to talk to the leaders of western countries, especially about nuclear weapons. In 1983 President Reagan of the United States called the Soviet Union an "evil empire." But in 1985 he held personal meetings with Mr. Gorbachev – and in Gorbachev's words, "the world had become a safer place." It seemed the Cold War was over. The map of Eastern Europe changed dramatically. East and West Germany were united as one country in 1990.

▲ *Cheering crowds from West and East Berlin celebrate on the Berlin Wall as the border is opened at midnight on November 9, 1989. This led to the reunification of Germany on October 3, 1990.*

▲ *Soviet leader Mikhail Gorbachev (right) and U.S. President Ronald Reagan establish friendly relations at the Reykjavik summit, Iceland, October 1986.*

▶ *In 1990, Solidarity's Lech Walesa was elected president of Poland.*

▼ *Boris Yeltsin defied a right-wing coup in August 1991 and became Russian leader.*

RUSSIAN FEDERATION

ESTONIA

LATVIA

LITHUANIA

• Gdansk
POLAND

Berlin •

• Prague
CZECH REPUBLIC

UKRAINE

SLOVAK REPUBLIC

• Budapest
HUNGARY

ROMANIA

GEORGIA

AZERBAIJAN

ARMENIA

YUGOSLAVIA

Sarajevo •

**The end of the
Cold War in
Eastern Europe.**

▲ *Unrest against Soviet rule flared in Estonia and the other Baltic States in 1990. Lithuania proclaimed her independence in that year. Latvia and Estonia followed in 1991.*

▶ *Gdansk dockyards were the center of the independent Polish trade union, Solidarity, led by Lech Walesa, which formed a freely elected government in Warsaw in 1989.*

1900
1905
Revolution in Russia

1910
1914
Archduke Ferdinand assassinated
1917
October Revolution
1918
Czar and family murdered

1920
1924
Stalin came to power

1930
1938
Germany partitions Czechoslovakia

1940
1943
Soviet victory at Stalingrad

1950
1953
Death of Stalin

1960
1968
Prague Spring Czechoslovakia

1970
1979
Soviet troops invade Afghanistan

1980
1985
Gorbachev becomes Soviet leader
1986
Nuclear power disaster Chernobyl

1990
1991
Soviet Union breaks up
1992
Civil war in Yugoslavia

JAPAN AND THE PACIFIC

▼ *Following savage fighting on the island of Iwo Jima between American marines and Japanese defenders, the American flag was hoisted by the victors on February 22, 1945.*

AFTER WORLD WAR II JAPAN LOST THE EMPIRE it had built up in Asia, and was occupied by American troops until 1952. America promoted Western-style ideas in government and society.

Hirohito was allowed to remain as emperor, but only as a political figurehead. The Allies were anxious to prevent the growth of Japanese military power, so the army and navy were demobilized and some war leaders were put on trial as war criminals. An attack was also made on the power of the zaibatsu, the big Japanese companies that had helped to run the war economy.

An economic miracle

The war left Japan in ruins, yet after 1950 an economic miracle took place. Strongly supported by government, industry was rebuilt. Measures were taken to make sure that Japanese goods were attractively priced and could compete well around the world.

With products like cameras, televisions, motorbikes, cars, calculators, and ships, Japan soon dominated world markets. Japanese firms invest heavily in research and development to come up with new products. They employ university-level business managers and concentrate on hi-tech industries like computers, televisions, and video equipment.

Big business

The Japanese economy has once again been dominated by large-scale business groups, including many that have become household names

▲ *The Japanese port of Hiroshima was hit by the first American atomic bomb on August 6, 1945, followed by Nagasaki on August 9. Both cities were totally destroyed and Japan surrendered.*

worldwide, such as Mitsubishi, Fuji, and Sony. Each group is involved in many different types of business, from banking to manufacturing or mining. Relations between employers and workers are traditionally very good. However, the Osaka earthquake in 1995 demonstrated the relative vulnerability of Japanese infrastructure.

▼ *Japan leads the world in pioneering robot technology. This is "Spider Robot," checking for cracks in a gas storage tank in 1994.*

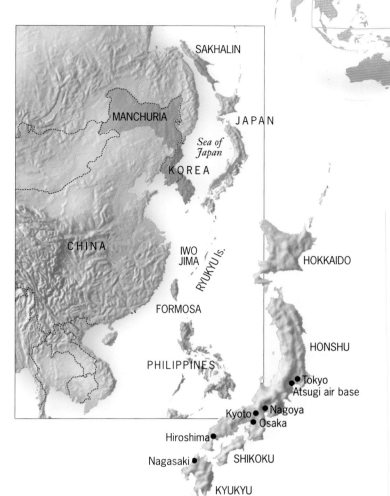

▲ *The Olympic Games were held in Tokyo in October 1964. The runner was a Japanese student who was born on August 6, 1945.*

SAKHALIN

MANCHURIA

JAPAN

Sea of Japan

KOREA

CHINA

HOKKAIDO

IWO JIMA

RYUKYU Is.

FORMOSA

HONSHU

PHILIPPINES

Tokyo
Atsugi air base

Kyoto • • Nagoya
• Osaka

Hiroshima •

Nagasaki • SHIKOKU

KYUKYU

Japan's recovery from the devastation of World War II.

███ Japan's manufacturing belt

▓▓▓ Japan's lost empire

▼ *Sumo wrestling, with its complex and mysterious rituals, is an ancient Japanese sport that is now attracting worldwide interest.*

1900
1904
Russo-Japanese War

1910
1910
Japan annexed Korea
1914
Japan entered World War I

1920
1926
Hirohito came to throne

1930
1931
Japan seized Manchuria from China
1937
Japan and China at war

1940
1945
Japan capitulates

1950
1952
Japan became independent

1960
1964
Olympic Games in Tokyo

1970
1970s
Japan becomes second largest economic power

1980
1989
Death of Hirohito

1990
1991
Japan world's largest donor of foreign aid

AUSTRALIA AND NEW ZEALAND

AUSTRALIA AND NEW ZEALAND traditionally had links with Britain and Europe, but World War II changed this. After the bombing of Pearl Harbor in 1941 there was a growing feeling that Australia and New Zealand were part of a Pacific community, where Japan could pose a formidable danger and America make a good ally. Australia and New Zealand joined forces with the U.S. in a defense agreement called ANZUS in 1951, and with other countries in the South East Asia Treaty Organization (SEATO) in 1954. New Zealand later followed its own line on nuclear defense, taking up a non-nuclear policy under Prime Minister David Lange (b.1942). Ancient cultures still exist in Australasia – the Maoris in New Zealand and

the Aborigines in Australia. In the 1980s and 1990s greater recognition was given to these peoples. Attention was focused on Aborginal problems by a mass demonstration in 1988, when Australia celebrated two hundred years of white settlement on the continent.

▲ *The Maoris were the original inhabitants of New Zealand but with the coming of European settlers their way of life was largely destroyed. However, they preserved their traditional dance, the Haka.*

▲ *Until the 1960s Aborigines were not considered Australian citizens. They were denied the vote and full social benefits and were not included in the census.*

The British connection

Australia changed its policy on immigration during the 1970s to accept newcomers from Asian countries, and trade links with Asia were promoted, especially after Britain joined the EEC in 1973. Japan is now an important trade partner, buying Australian iron ore and coal, as well as investing in property. The Commonwealth tie with Britain remains and Queen Elizabeth II (b.1926) is still head of state in both countries. In more recent years this has led to Australian protest. Sport is a less controversial part of the British tradition. Soccer became popular after 1945; cricket, tennis, golf, and rugby have all produced sporting superstars, from Evonne Goolagong to Greg Norman.

Loosening of Australia's links with Europe and the forging of new ones with Asia.

▼ The newly-crowned Queen Elizabeth toured Australia with Prince Philip in 1954. The Queen opened the South Australian Parliament in Adelaide in March. Everywhere the royal couple were greeted by cheering crowds.

▼ The Aborigines are the indigenous inhabitants of Australia. Recently, attempts have been made to protect their rights from non-native encroachment.

1900
1901
Commonwealth of Australia set up
1907
New Zealand became a dominion

1910
1910
First Australian coins minted
1911
Universal military training in New Zealand

1920
1927
Canberra new capital

1930
1931
Australia & New Zealand became independent dominions

1940
1941
John Cutin becomes prime minister

1950
1951
ANZUS defense agreement signed
1954
SEATO defense agreement signed

1960
1962
Australia commits to Vietnam War
1966
Australia adopts decimal currency

1970
1973
Sydney Opera House opened
1979
"White Australia" policy abolished

1980
1984
New Zealand declared nuclear-free zone

1990
1992
Fishing rights granted to Maoris

CHINA

U NDER THE LEADERSHIP OF CHAIRMAN Mao Zedong, who led the communists to victory after the defeat of Japan, China concentrated on economic and social reform. It was a time of great idealism. In 1958 Mao launched a new economic program known as "The Great Leap Forward," which aimed to transform China from a poor farming country into a modern industrial nation by setting up small rural industries and cooperative farms called communes. Political struggle again took place in the 1960s. Fanatical young supporters of Mao, called the Red Guard, executed, imprisoned, and shamed anyone suspected of disagreeing with Mao's ideas. This period, known as the Cultural Revolution, lasted from 1965–1969.

Foreign relations

China's attitude toward the outside world has been wary. Disputes with Russia came to the fore in the late 1950s after earlier cooperation. China had always been suspicious of the West, especially America, but this changed with the visit of President Richard Nixon in 1972. Student calls for democracy in Tiananmen Square, Beijing, in 1989, were put down with tanks, and thousands of protesters were killed. The 1990s, however, have generally seen more economic freedom, as China opens up to world trade and visits by foreign tourists.

▲ *Worried about growing numbers, China's officials urge parents to have only one child. But many families ignore this advice.*

◀ *In 1974 workers in China came face to face with China's ancient past when they discovered these terracotta warriors.*

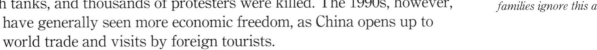

▶ *Red Guards, young supporters of Chairman Mao, went to extreme lengths to uphold Mao's ideals. Children were given names such as "Protect Mao" when they were born.*

USSR

CHINA

TIBET

Beijing •

NORTH
KOREA

SOUTH
KOREA

Shanghai •

Pacific Ocean

TAIWAN

HONG KONG

NORTH
VIETNAM

PHILIPPINES

*South China
Sea*

SOUTH
VIETNAM

**After the Cultural
Revolution, China
began to open up
to the West.**

▼ *Hong Kong, which
becomes part of China
again in 1997, is a
leading international
business center.*

▲ *Four million bicycles take to
the streets each day in the city
of Shanghai, as commuters
head for work.*

1900
1898-1900
Boxer Revolution
1908
Death of Chinese
Emperor

1910
1911
Sun Yat-sen president
Nationalist revolution
1912
Kuomintang set up
1918
Mao Zedong forms
Chinese Communist Party

1920
1927
Civil War

1930
1935
End of Long March

1940
1949
Mao proclaims People's
Republic of China

1950
1958
Great Leap Forward

1960
1965-9
Cultural Revolution

1970
1976
Death of Mao

1980
1989
Tiananmen Square
riots

1990
1992
Trials of pro-democracy
activists

SOUTHERN ASIA

IDNIGHT ON AUGUST 14, 1947 saw the end of British rule in India. India became a symbol of hope for other nations seeking independence. In the Dutch East Indies, for example, nationalists under Dr. Sukarno (1901–1970) struggled for freedom, achieving independence as Indonesia in 1949. Ceylon became independent in 1947 – though it remained part of the British Commonwealth, and was renamed Sri Lanka in 1972.

Indian independence

There were great celebrations to mark Indian independence, and also bloodshed. The mainly Hindu Congress controled most areas, but the Punjab and Bengal were mainly Muslim. Demands for a separate Muslim state resulted in the country being partitioned to create the new state of Pakistan. Over six million Muslims left the Punjab for Pakistan. The Indian national leader, Mohandas Gandhi, was assassinated in 1948.

Relations between India and Pakistan broke down in a dispute over the state of Kashmir, where the Maharaja was a Hindu but the great majority of his subjects were Muslims. In 1971 civil war broke out between East and West Pakistan. Aided by India, East Pakistan won independence and was renamed Bangladesh.

▲ *The Golden Temple at Amritsar, India, was the scene of disturbance in 1984 when Indira Gandhi ordered troops into this Sikh holy place.*

Political assassination

In India, too, there was unrest. In the Punjab, Sikh calls for independence brought clashes with troops. Prime Minister Indira Gandhi (1917–1984) was killed by Sikh extremists in 1984. The Indian and Pakistan economies have grown since independence. Agricultural output has been boosted by the "green revolution" in crops and fertilizers. Industry has also developed. By 1994 increasing Asian prosperity had made the area one of the world's fastest growing markets.

◄ *Political feeling in Asia mounted after World War II. But the years since independence have not always been smooth. Unrest is felt as ethnic minorities champion their rights in Assam and Tamil Nadu.*

KASHMIR
(disputed territory)

WEST PAKISTAN

PUNJAB

Amritsar

Delhi

Indus River

NEPAL

Karachi

Ganges River

INDIA

ASSAM

BENGAL
Dacca

Bombay

HYDERABAD

Calcutta

EAST PAKISTAN
(became Bangladesh in 1971)

CEYLON
(Sri Lanka after 1972)

New dimensions of the Indian subcontinent.

■ Border of British India, 1939
■ Border of Independent India, 1947
■ East and West Pakistan, 1947
■ States not included in 1947 partition

◀ Snaking through 500 miles of harsh terrain between Pakistan and China, the Karakoram Highway was finished in 1978.

◀ A great leap forward was made in farming, thanks to new ideas known as the "green revolution."

▲ Calcutta's inhabitants line up in the street for medical treatment. In 1994 a plague epidemic broke out in India.

1900
1901 Famine in India
1905 Muslim League founded

1910
1911 Durbar, King George V crowned
1919 Amritsar massacre

1920
1920 Gandhi's non-cooperation movement founded

1930
1931 Conference on Indian home rule

1940
1947 Indian independence
1948 Mohandas Gandhi killed

1950
1951-2 Election of Congress Party

1960
1966 Indira Gandhi becomes prime minister

1970
1971 Indo-Pakistan War

1980
1984 Indira Gandhi killed
1988 Benazir Bhutto prime minister

1990
1994 Plague in India

VIETNAM, CAMBODIA, AND LAOS

IN WORLD WAR II, JAPAN OVERRAN Vietnam, Cambodia, and Laos. After the War, French control was reasserted, but there were strong nationalist movements. In Vietnam, the Viet Minh fought for independence, defeating France at Dien Bien Phu in 1954. Cambodia became independent in 1953, and Laos in 1954.

War in Vietnam

More fighting was to come when Vietnam was divided in 1954. The North was communist under Ho Chi Minh (1890–1969), and in the South a government was set up under Ngo Dinh Diem (1901–1963), supported by the United States. American involvement grew. At first U.S. military advisers were sent to South Vietnam, then troops followed in 1965. The Vietcong, who fought the South Vietnamese and U.S. forces, were supplied from North Vietnam along the Ho Chi Minh trail. U.S. troops were gradually pulled out after 1971, but civil war continued until 1975, when Saigon fell to North Vietnam and North and South were united.

▲ *Helicopters were vital to America's war in Vietnam. "Choppers" helped to move troops and rescue the injured.*

▲ *In the Vietnam War, the North was aided by communist China and the Soviet Union, while the South was given aid by the U.S.*

The Khmer Rouge

In 1975 the communist Khmer Rouge movement took power in Cambodia, or Kampuchea, as it was renamed. Millions died under the brutal regime of Pol Pot (b.1926). Vietnam invaded Kampuchea in 1978 and Pol Pot was thrown from power in 1979.

▶ *The Vietnam War became unpopular in the U.S., particularly with students, and this led to demonstrations like this one in New York City.*

86

▲ *Tragedy came to Cambodia when the Khmer Rouge under leader Pol Pot tried to create a communist society.*

The Ho Chi Minh Trail through Laos and Cambodia.

▬▬▬ Ho Chi Minh Trail

CHINA

River Mekong

Dien Bien Phu
Hanoi
Gulf of Tonkin
NORTH VIETNAM

Luang Prabang

Vientiane

LAOS

THAILAND

SOUTH VIETNAM

Phnom Penh
CAMBODIA
(renamed Kampuchea)

Saigon
(renamed Ho Chi Minh City)

1900
1908
Nationalist movement in French Indochina prompted by Tonkin uprising

1910
1914
Attempted assassination of French governor of Indochina

1920
1925
Nationalist riots in Hanoi

1930
1930
Ho Chi Minh founds Indochinese Communist Party

1940
1945
Vietminh take Saigon

1950
1953
Cambodia gains independence
1954
French defeated at Dien Bien Phu

1960
1964-75
Vietnam War

1970
1975
Khmer Rouge take power

1980
1989
Troops leave Cambodia

1990
1992
Foreign investment allowed

AFRICA

A WIND OF CHANGE SWEPT through Africa after World War II. France gave up Morocco and Tunisia in 1956. In 1957 Britain gave up the Gold Coast, and it took the name Ghana under Prime Minister Kwame Nkrumah (1909–72). These were pioneering days, but by 1966 most of Africa had won its freedom. Rhodesia was renamed Zimbabwe in 1980.

In the 1950s and 1960s progress was made in establishing industries, providing power by hydroelectric projects, improving healthcare, and setting up schools.

▲ *The British flag is lowered for the last time in Rhodesia, Britain's last African colony. Rhodesia was reborn as Zimbabwe.*

The end of apartheid

In South Africa the harsh system of discrimination against the blacks known as "apartheid" remained. In 1990, ANC leader Nelson Mandela (b.1918) was set free after over twenty-five years in prison, and talks began with President F.W. de Klerk (b.1936). In 1994 the first elections at which blacks as well as whites could vote took place, and Mandela became South Africa's first black president, with de Klerk as vice president in a Government of National Unity.

Famine and disease

People left the countryside for the city life, but for many, this meant grim conditions in makeshift shelters on the city fringe. Disease, especially AIDS, now presents problems in many African countries. There is also the constant threat of drought and famine, as happened in Ethiopia in the 1980s. Outbreaks of tribal violence, as in Rwanda in 1994 and 1995, killed thousands, with many more dying as starvation and cholera broke out in the refugee camps in neighboring countries.

▲ *Apartheid ruled South African life until recently. The word comes from the Afrikaan language and means "separateness." Blacks and whites were separated in work, education, and leisure.*

▶ *The Kylie Dam in Zimbabwe is one of many hydroelectric power stations built by the new African nations.*

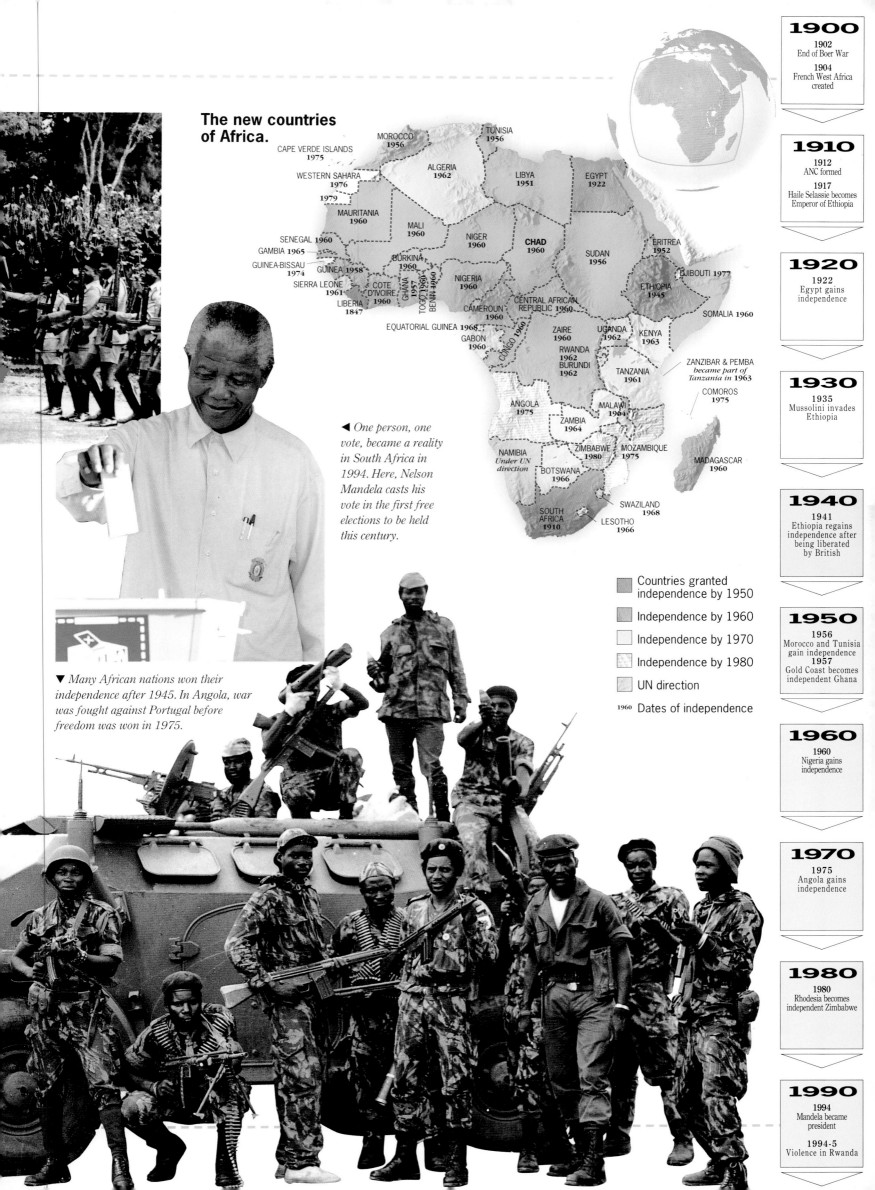

The new countries of Africa.

CAPE VERDE ISLANDS
1975

MOROCCO
1956

TUNISIA
1956

ALGERIA
1962

LIBYA
1951

EGYPT
1922

WESTERN SAHARA
1976
1979

MAURITANIA
1960

MALI
1960

NIGER
1960

CHAD
1960

SUDAN
1956

ERITREA
1952

SENEGAL *1960*

GAMBIA *1965*

GUINEA-BISSAU
1974

GUINEA *1958*

BURKINA
1960

SIERRA LEONE
1961

COTE
D'IVOIRE
1960

GHANA *1957*

TOGO *1960*

BENIN *1960*

NIGERIA
1960

DJIBOUTI *1977*

ETHIOPIA
1945

LIBERIA
1847

CENTRAL AFRICAN
REPUBLIC *1960*

CAMEROUN
1960

SOMALIA *1960*

EQUATORIAL GUINEA *1968*

GABON
1960

CONGO *1960*

ZAIRE
1960

UGANDA
1962

KENYA
1963

RWANDA
1962

BURUNDI
1962

TANZANIA
1961

ZANZIBAR & PEMBA
*became part of
Tanzania in 1963*

COMOROS
1975

ANGOLA
1975

MALAWI
1964

ZAMBIA
1964

MADAGASCAR
1960

NAMIBIA
*Under UN
direction*

ZIMBABWE
1980

MOZAMBIQUE
1975

BOTSWANA
1966

SWAZILAND
1968

SOUTH
AFRICA
1910

LESOTHO
1966

◄ *One person, one vote, became a reality in South Africa in 1994. Here, Nelson Mandela casts his vote in the first free elections to be held this century.*

▼ *Many African nations won their independence after 1945. In Angola, war was fought against Portugal before freedom was won in 1975.*

■ Countries granted independence by 1950

■ Independence by 1960

□ Independence by 1970

▨ Independence by 1980

▨ UN direction

1960 Dates of independence

1900
1902
End of Boer War
1904
French West Africa created

1910
1912
ANC formed
1917
Haile Selassie becomes Emperor of Ethiopia

1920
1922
Egypt gains independence

1930
1935
Mussolini invades Ethiopia

1940
1941
Ethiopia regains independence after being liberated by British

1950
1956
Morocco and Tunisia gain independence
1957
Gold Coast becomes independent Ghana

1960
1960
Nigeria gains independence

1970
1975
Angola gains independence

1980
1980
Rhodesia becomes independent Zimbabwe

1990
1994
Mandela became president
1994-5
Violence in Rwanda

THE MIDDLE EAST

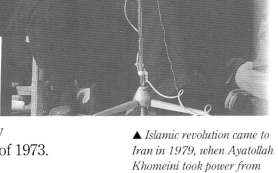

A HANDSHAKE BETWEEN LEADERS Yitzhak Rabin of Israel and Palestinian Yasir Arafat (b.1929) in 1993 seemed to bring peace closer to the divided Middle East. The new Jewish state of Israel was set up in 1948 and war with the Arabs followed. Israel expanded into Arab-held territory, notably in the Sinai Campaign of 1956 and the Six Day War of 1967. In 1964 the Palestine Liberation Organization (PLO) was formed to challenge Israel's presence in former Palestine. In 1979 agreement was finally reached with President Sadat of Egypt after the Yom Kippur War of 1973.

▲ *Islamic revolution came to Iran in 1979, when Ayatollah Khomeini took power from the Shah. He ruled Iran as a hard-line Islamic country.*

War and peace

In 1993–1994 a breakthrough brought understanding between Israel and the PLO, and paved the way forward for a handover of power in Gaza, Jericho, and the West Bank. Talks began which have brought peace between Israel and Jordan, and may bring peace between Israel and Syria.

A renewal of the Islamic faith has taken place in the Middle East. Revolution in Iran in 1979 brought the fundamentalist religious leader, Ayatollah Khomeini, to power. He generated intense anti-Western feeling, and encouraged a return to traditional Islamic ideas about women's place in society. War between Iran and Iraq broke out in 1980 and lasted until 1988. A dispute triggered by the Iraqi invasion of Kuwait flared into the Gulf War in 1991, with U.S. and other foreign involvement.

▲ *During the Gulf War hundreds of oil wells burned out of control, having been set on fire by the Iraqi forces.*

▶ *In 1994 Israel's Yitzhak Rabin and Yasir Arafat of the PLO made history by reaching a peace settlement. The turning point in the peace process came in talks with President Sadat of Egypt in 1979.*

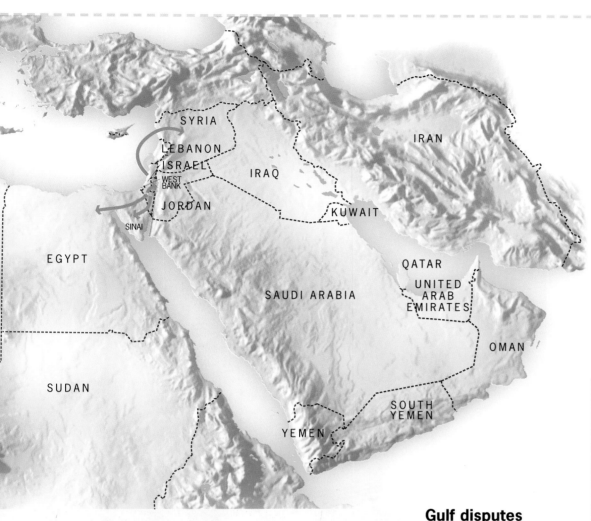

SYRIA
LEBANON
ISRAEL
WEST BANK
JORDAN
SINAI
EGYPT
SUDAN
IRAN
IRAQ
KUWAIT
QATAR
UNITED ARAB EMIRATES
SAUDI ARABIA
OMAN
YEMEN
SOUTH YEMEN

Conflicts in the Middle East since World War II.

- Israel invades Sinai, 1956
- Israel invades Syria, West Bank, and Egypt, 1967
- Israel invades Lebanon, 1967 and 1982

LEBANON
ISRAEL
IRAQ
Tehran
Shatt al Arab Waterway
IRAN

Gulf disputes 1990-1991.

Iraq invades Iran, 1980; Kuwait, 1990

◀ *For much of this century, the Middle East has been torn by war between the Arabs and the Israelis.*

▼ *Mecca, the holy city of Islam, is visited by thousands of pilgrims. A revival of Islam has taken place in many parts of Africa, Asia, and the Middle East.*

1900
1902
Ibn Saud captures Riyadh, Saudi Arabia
1908
Pan-Islamic movement begins in Turkey

1910
1917
Balfour Declaration

1920
1923
Republic of Turkey created

1930
1930
Iraq gains independence
1932
Saudi Arabia established

1940
1948
Jewish state of Israel comes into existence

1950
1957
Sinai Campaign

1960
1964
PLO formed
1967
Six Day War

1970
1973
Yom Kippur War
1979
Ayatollah Khomeini takes power in Iran

1980
1980
War between Iran and Iraq
1982
Israel invades Lebanon

1990
1991
Gulf War broke out
1994
Peace settlement

THE WAY OF THE WORLD

CANADA

UNITED STATES

CALIFORNIA

BRAZIL

Most countries in the world have prospered since 1945. In Asia, Africa, and Latin America, however, population growth has soared, and this reduces living standards. The contrast between wealthy, industrial, developed nations and poor nations has been particularly apparent since 1973, when oilproducing nations in the Middle East, like Saudi Arabia, raised the price of oil worldwide. This brought recession that lasted into the 1980s. For Third World countries like Brazil, Zaire, and Sudan, this meant greater borrowing, but many were already struggling to make repayments. Aid had to be arranged to cope with this crisis.

In developed countries, the 1980s were boom years. Computer technology, based on the silicon chip, produced a revolution in manufacturing, in offices, even, thanks to electronic bar codes, at supermarket checkouts. In California's Silicon Valley, the microcomputer was pioneered by Apple. Japan then led the way in new developments. Governments that wanted to boost new enterprises, but without direct state involvement, were elected in the U.S. and Britain. The service industry also developed and prospered.

Toward the new century

World recession bit again in 1990, causing even powerful economies like Japan to cut back and restructure. However, growing markets in eastern Europe and especially in Asia, seem to many to point to future prosperity. At the end of the 20th century, there is a feeling of world community that did not exist at the start of the century. Teenagers around the world buy the same jeans, soft drinks, and listen to music from pop stars. There is increasing concern about the environment and greater awareness of the problems of providing enough food for all the people in the world, as well as tackling killer diseases like AIDS. By the 21st century, with new computer revolutions like the development of the Internet, the members of the world community will increasingly be talking to each other by computer, too.

▲ *Today, male and female students across the world effect a universal dress code of jeans and T-shirts, and listen to the same music, all inspired by American examples.*

▶ *Japan, Singapore, Taiwan, and South Korea have led the world in developing electronic technology. Here, an operative in Singapore's Social Development Unit demonstrates Tele-Pal, an electronic dating system.*

RUSSIA

GREAT
BRITAIN

UKRAINE
• Chernobyl

JAPAN

SOUTH KOREA

TAIWAN

SAUDI
ARABIA

AFRICA

INDIA

SUDAN

INDONESIA

ZAIRE

AUSTRALIA

NEW ZEALAND

**The changing
face of the
world at the end
of the 20th
century.**

Population boom

New markets

▼ *Bob Geldof and fellow
singers hold a concert on
behalf of Live Aid, a
global charity.*

▲ *In 1986 the nuclear
power station at
Chernobyl in Ukraine blew
up, contaminating large
areas of Russia and
Western Europe. The
disaster was marked by its
incompetent handling by
the Soviet authorities.*

Index

A

Aborigines 80, 81
Abyssinia 54
  see also Ethiopia
advertising 58
Africa 24-5, 32, 54-5, 88-9
African National Congress (ANC) 24, 88
agriculture 10, 16, 17, 18, 22, 46, 48, 50
AIDS 88, 92
airplanes 9, 48, 58
Alberta 8
Allende, Salvador 72
Allied Powers 62, 63, 64, 68, 78
America, Central 10-11, 40-1
America, Southern 10-11, 40-1, 72-3
Amritsar 52, 84
Angola 89
ANZUS 80
apartheid 88
Arafat, Yasir 90, 91
Argentina 10, 60, 72
Armstrong, Louis 38
arts 12, 48
Asia Minor 56
  see also Turkey
Asia, Southern 22-3, 52-3, 84-5
Assam 84
Ataturk
  see Kemal, Mustafa
atomic bomb, the 64, 65
Australia 18-19, 32, 48-9, 80-1
Austria 60
Austria-Hungary 28, 31, 36
Axis Powers 62, 63
Azikiwe, Nnandi 54

B

Balfour Declaration 56
Balkan Wars 28
Baltic States 77
Bangladesh 84
Battle of Britain 64
Bauhaus 12
Beatles, the 75
Belgium 12, 29, 32, 34, 42, 54, 64
Bell, Alexander Graham 27
Bengal 22
Berlin 68-9, 76
Bismarck, Otto von 30
Blitzkrieg 64
Boer War 24, 25
Bolivia 40, 41, 72
Bolsheviks 14, 30, 44
Bosnia-Herzegovina 14, 28
Boxer Revolution 20, 21
Brasilia 72
Brazil 10, 40, 41, 72, 92
Britain 12, 13, 18, 19, 22, 24, 25, 28, 29, 30, 32, 34, 36, 42, 47, 48, 52, 54, 56, 60, 62, 64, 66, 88
British Commonwealth 18, 48, 80, 84
British Empire 18, 22, 23
Brusilov, Aleksey 30
Bulgaria 68
Burma 52, 64

C

Cambodia 86, 87
Cameroons 54
Canada 8-9, 38-9, 70-1
Canberra 19
Canton 20, 50
Cárdenas, Lázaro 40
car industry 38, 70
Caroline Islands 46
Castro, Fidel 72
Ceylon 52, 84
Chaco War 40, 41
Channel Tunnel 74
Che Guevara 72
chemical industry 12, 26

Chiang Kai-shek 50
Chile 10, 72
China 16, 20-1, 46, 50-1, 66, 82
Churchill, Winston 62, 68
civil rights movement 70-1
Clemenceau, Georges 30, 36
coal 12, 26
Cockcroft, J. D. 59
Cold War 68-9
colonialism 24-5
communism 44, 50, 52, 60, 61, 68, 72, 76, 82
concentration camps 66-7
Concorde 74
Constantinople 56
Contras 72
copper 10
Cuba 68, 72
Curie, Marie 12
Cultural Revolution 82
Cyprus 74
Czechoslovakia 36, 60, 68, 76

D

D-Day landings 64
de Gaulle, Charles 62
de Klerk, F. W. 88
Denmark 64
Depression 38, 39, 42, 43, 48, 58
Diaz, Porfirio 11
dictators 10
Dube, J. W. 24
Dutch East Indies 52, 84

E

Easter Rising 42, 43
Egypt 24, 56, 64, 90
Eisenhower, Dwight D. 70
electricity industry 12, 26

Elizabeth II, Queen of England 80, 81
Estonia 36, 77
Ethiopia 24, 88
  see also Abyssinia
Europe, Eastern 14-15, 42-3, 76-7
Europe, Western 12-13, 42-3, 74-5
European Economic Community 74

F

fascism 60, 61
Ferdinand, Archduke of Austria-Hungary 14, 28
Finland 36
Foch, Ferdinand 30
France 24, 28, 29, 30, 32, 36, 42, 54, 56, 60, 62, 64, 68, 88
Franco, General 60

G

Gallipoli campaign 32, 48
Gandhi, Indira 84
Gandhi, Mohandas 52, 84
Gaza 90
George V, King of England 23, 31
Germany 12, 24, 28, 29, 30, 31, 32, 34, 36, 42, 43, 44, 48, 54, 60, 62, 64, 66, 68, 76
Ghana 88
Gold Coast 54, 55, 88
Golden Gate Bridge 38, 39
Gomez, Juan 10
Gorbachev, Mikhail 76
Greece 64
green revolution 84, 85
Guam 8

Guatemala 72
Gulf War 90

H

Haile Selassie 54
Hawaii 8
Hirohito, Emperor of Japan 46, 47, 62, 78
Hiroshima 64, 78
Hitler, Adolf 42, 60, 62, 63, 64
Ho Chi Minh 52, 53, 60, 86, 87
Hong Kong 20, 83
Hungary 68, 69

I

immigration 8, 9
India 22-3, 24, 32, 36, 52-3, 84-5
Indian National Congress 52
Indochina 22, 52
Indonesia 84
industry 9, 12, 16, 18, 22, 26, 38, 46, 50, 72, 74, 78
inflation 36, 42
Internet 92
Iran 56, 90
Iraq 36, 56, 90
  see also Persia
Ireland 42, 43
iron industry 12, 16, 26
Israel 56, 90
Istanbul
  see Constantinople
Italy 24, 28, 42, 54, 60, 62, 64
Iwo Jima 78

J

Japan 14, 16-17, 32, 46-7, 62, 64, 66, 78-9, 80, 82, 86, 92
Jericho 90
Jews 56, 62, 66

Jinnah, Mohammed Ali 52
Johnson, Lyndon B. 70
Jordan 56, 90

K

Kampuchea
    see Cambodia
Karafuto 16
Karakorum Highway 85
Kemal, Mustafa 56, 57
Kennedy, John F. 70
Kenya 24
Khmer Rouge 86, 87
Khomeini, Ayatollah 90
King, Martin Luther 70, 71
Kitchener, Lord 34
Korea 16, 46, 66
Korean War 68
Kuomintang 21, 50
Kuwait 90

L

Labor movement 18
Lange, David 80
Laos 86, 87
Latvia 77
Laurel and Hardy 58
League of Nations 36, 46, 48, 54, 56
Lebanon 36, 56
Lenin, Vladimir Ilyich 44
Libya 24
Lithuania 77
Lloyd George, David 30, 34, 36
Long March 50, 51
Lusitania 31, 34

M

Malaya 65
Manchu dynasty 20
Manchuria 16, 46, 50
mandates 36, 54, 55
Mandela, Nelson 88, 89
Mansfield, Katherine 48
Mao Zedong 50, 51, 82
Maoris 80
Marconi, Guglielmo 12
Mariana Islands 46
Marshall Islands 46
Marshall Plan 74
Marx, Karl 14
Masai people 24

Melbourne 19
Mexican Revolution 11
Mexico 11, 40, 41, 72
mining industry 8, 10, 18
Mondrian, Piet 12
Morocco 24, 88
movies 38, 58, 71
music 38, 75
Muslim League 22, 52
Mussolini, Benito 42, 43, 60, 62
Mutsuhito, Emperor of China 16

N

Nagasaki 64, 78
National Association for the Advancement of Colored People 8
nationalism 10, 14, 20, 22, 24, 28, 50, 54, 84
Nazism 42, 60, 62, 66
Nehru, Jawaharlal 52, 60
Netherlands 64
New York 58
New Zealand 18-19, 32, 48-9, 80-1
Newfoundland 70
Ngo Dinh Diem 86
Nicaragua 10
Nicholas II, Czar 14, 15, 30
Nixon, Richard 82
Nkrumah, Kwame 88
North Atlantic Treaty Organization (NATO) 74
Norway 64
nuclear power 76, 92

O

October Revolution 44
oil industry 8, 10, 40, 70, 92
Olympic Games 79
Ottoman Empire 28, 32, 36

P

Pakistan 84
Palestine 36, 56, 90
Palestine Liberation Organization (PLO) 90
Panama Canal 11
Paraguay 40, 41
Passchendaele, Battle of 32

Pearl Harbor 61, 62, 64, 80
Péron, Juan 60, 72
Persia 24
    see also Iran
Peru 73
Philippines 8
Pinochet, Augusto 72
Pol Pot 86, 87
Poland 36, 60, 68, 76
pollution 7
population growth 12, 13, 16, 26, 70, 92
Portugal 10, 54
Potsdam 68
Princip, Gavrilo 28
prohibition 38

Q

Quebec 70

R

Rabin, Yitzhak 90
radio 7, 12, 58
railroads 16, 22, 40
rainforests 72, 73
Rathenau, Walter 34
Reagan, Ronald 76
recession 92
Rhodesia 88
Rivera, Diego 40, 41
Romania 76
Roosevelt, F. D. 38, 39, 62, 68
Roosevelt, Theodore "Teddy" 8
Russia 14-15, 16, 28, 30, 31, 44-5, 62, 64, 82
    see also Soviet Union
Russian Revolution 14, 30, 44-5
Russo-Japanese War 14, 16
Rutherford, Ernest 48, 59
Rwanda 88
Rwanda-Urundi 54

S

Sadat, President of Egypt 90
Sarajevo 14, 28
Saskatchewan 8
Saudi Arabia 36, 56, 92
Schlieffen, Alfred von Graf 29, 30, 32
Schlieffen Plan 31, 32

SEATO 80
Serbia 28, 31
Sinai Campaign 90
Singapore 65, 92
Six Day War 90
social reform 8, 12, 16, 18, 40, 70, 74
Solidarity 76, 77
Somalia 24
Somme, Battle of the 32
South Africa 54, 88
South Korea 92
Soviet Union 60, 68, 76
    see also Russia
Spain 10, 24, 42, 60
Sri Lanka 84
    see also Ceylon
Stalin, Joseph 44, 45, 60, 62, 68
Stopes, Dr. Marie 42
strikes 12, 42
Sudan 92
Suez Canal 24
suffragettes 13
Sukarno, Dr. 84
Sumatra 22
Sun Yat-sen 20, 21, 50
Syria 36, 56, 90

T

Taiping rebellion 20
Taiwan 46, 92
Tamil Nadu 84
Tanganyika (Tanzania) 54
technology 12, 26, 58, 92
television 7, 48, 58, 76
textile industry 12, 16, 22, 26
Thatcher, Margaret 74
Tiananmen Square 82
Tirpitz, Alfred von 30
Togo 54
Tokyo 17
trade 16, 74
Trans-Siberian Railroad 15
treaty ports 20, 50
Triple Entente 28, 35
Trotsky, Leon 44
Tunisia 88
Turkey 48, 56, 57

U

unemployment 58, 59
UNESCO 74
United Nations 74

United States 8-9, 34, 38-9, 61, 62, 64, 68, 70-1, 72, 74, 78, 80

V

Vargas, Getúlio 40, 41
Venezuela 10
Verdun, Battle of 32
Versailles, Treaty of 36, 48, 60
Victoria, Queen of England 12
Vietnam 86-7
voting 8, 13, 18

W

Walesa, Lech 76, 77
Wall Street Crash 38, 58
Walton, Ernest S. 59
West Bank 90
Western Front 32, 33
wheat 8, 10, 48
White, Patrick 48
Wilhelm II, Kaiser 30
Wilson, Woodrow 30, 31, 36, 37
women's rights 8, 13, 18, 42
World Health Organization (WHO) 74
Wright, Orville and Wilbur 9

Y

Yalta 68
Yamamoto, Isoroku 62
Yeltsin, Boris 76
Yom Kippur War 90
Yugoslavia 36

Z

Zaire 92
Zelaya, José 10
Zimbabwe 88

Acknowledgments

Quarto would like to thank the following for providing photographs,
and for granting permission to reproduce copyright material.

(b = bottom, c = center, l = left, r = right, t = top)

E.T. Archive: 41bl; *Hulton/Apple*: 75br; *Hulton-Deutsch Collection Ltd*: 1r, 6t, 8tr, 8cl, 9br, 10bl, 11cl, 12tr, 12cl, 12br, 13bl, 14tr, 14bl, 14/15bc/r, 15cr, 16tr, 16bl, 17bl, 17br, 18cl, 19cl, 20/21c, 20bl, 21br, 22tr, 23b, 26br, 27bc, 27bl, 28tr, 28cr, 28br, 29cl, 29b, 30tr, 30cl, 30bcl, 30/31bc, 31cr, 32tr, 32cr, 33br, 34cr, 34bl, 35b, 36, 37, 39br, 40tr, 42bl, 43cr, 43br, 44tr, 44cl, 45bl, 47br, 48br, 49b, 52tr, 52bl, 53c, 54tr, 54c, 54bl, 56bl, 58, 59c, 60/61bc, 62cr, 63b, 64bl, 65bl, 65br, 66tr, 66bl, 66/67cb, 67br, 68tr, 68bl, 68/69cb, 69br, 69cr, 72bl, 74/75cb, 79tl, 80bl, 80/81bc, 82br, 86tr, 86c, 86/87b, 88/89b, 91cl; *Hulton/Reuters*: 89cl, 90/91cb; Life File: 2/3, 19b, 39bl, 74tr (*E. Lee*), 88cl (*S. Davie*), 92cr (*D. Thompson*); *Robert Opie*: 27br, 67cr; *Popperfoto*: 4, 6b, 11br, 12cr, 14cr, 18tr, 20tr, 22cl, 22br, 24tr, 24cl, 24/25b, 31cl, 32/33bc, 34tr, 35cr, 38tr, 38bl, 38bl, 41tl, 42tr, 42/43c, 45br, 46tr, 46/47bc, 50tr, 50bl, 51bl, 53b, 55b, 56tr, 57br, 59br, 59bl, 60tr, 60bl, 62tr, 62br, 62bl, 64tr, 70tr, 70bl, 71cl, 71bl, 71br, 73br, 74bl, 76cl, 78tr, 78bl, 79bl, 79br, 80tr, 84bl, 88/89tc, 90cl, 92br, 93br; *Range/Bettmann*: 8/9bc, 40b, 41br;TRIP: 6c, 74/75c (*N. Moseley*), 7, 76b (*D. Oliver*), 10/11tc (*W. Jacobs*), 51br, 82bl (*K. Cardwell*), 55tl, 84/85tc, 85cl (*H. Rogers*), 73/73tc (*M. Dubin*), 73cl (*J.Highet*), 76tr (*M. O'Brien-Thumm*), 76cr (*M.Jenkin*), 77bl (*T. Nooris*), 77br (*M. Barlow*), 81br (*Eye Ubiquitous*), 82tr (*F. Good*), 83bl (*C. Thradgold*), 84/85bc (*B. Gibbs*), 85cl (*D. Burrows*), 87tl (*J. Wakelin*), 88bc (*J. Short*), 93cl (*V. Shuba*), 57bl, 61br, 83br, 90tr, 91br.